Generative AI in Higher Education

Adebowale Owoseni · Oluwaseun Kolade ·
Abiodun Egbetokun

Generative AI in Higher Education

Innovation Strategies for Teaching and Learning

palgrave
macmillan

Adebowale Owoseni
School of Computer Science
and Informatics
De Montfort University
Leicester, UK

Oluwaseun Kolade
Sheffield Business School
Sheffield Hallam University
Sheffield, UK

Abiodun Egbetokun
Leicester Castle Business School
De Montfort University
Leicester, UK

ISBN 978-3-031-60178-1 ISBN 978-3-031-60179-8 (eBook)
https://doi.org/10.1007/978-3-031-60179-8

This Palgrave Macmillan imprint is published by the registered company Springer Nature Switzerland AG
The registered company address is: Gewerbestrasse 11, 6330 Cham, Switzerland

Acknowledgments

This book represents a collective effort, a journey undertaken by three passionate authors—Adebowale, Oluwaseun, and Abiodun—who are committed to exploring the transformative potential of generative AI in education. Our combined experiences, insights, and dedication have brought this work to life, and we are immensely grateful to the individuals and teams that have supported us along the way.

Adebowale extends his deepest gratitude to God, the giver of life! Special appreciation goes to his wife, Debbie, and their children, Divine, Fifi, and Zion, for their encouragement and for enduring the inevitable sacrifices. Your support has been invaluable. He also thanks his students and colleagues at De Montfort University, particularly the Centre for Computing and Social Responsibility (CCSR) and the Centre for Academic Innovation and Teaching Excellence (CAITE), for providing the opportunity to lead discussions that highlighted the importance of this book. Additionally, he expresses heartfelt gratitude to his family, friends and mentors who have steadfastly supported his pracademic and research career. To the Envoy Nation and Envoy Academic Expression, thank you for the privilege of influencing many through my diverse expressions.

Oluwaseun is grateful for his wife, Ore, and daughter, Demi, for their understanding and support, as he took time away to give attention to this book. He is also thankful for the various interactions that have shaped aspects of this work, including with students and colleagues from Sheffield

Hallam University, colleagues from African Scholars' Forum, and participants in the British Council Research Connect workshops, among others. He also expresses his thanks to Olamide, of Enterprise Republic, for his admin support; and to all the family and friends who continue to encourage and support his research in the field of generative AI.

Abiodun thanks his wife, Oluwatosin, and children, Testimony, Oluwasemiloore and Barnabas, for their understanding and encouragement which have been a constant source of motivation. He is grateful for the intellectual stimulation and constructive feedback from students and colleagues at De Montfort University, National Centre for Technology Management, African Institute for Science Policy and Innovation, AfricaLICS and NigeriaLICS, among others. He also thanks the family, friends and mentors through whose support he has come this far.

Collectively, we thank the reviewers and all who took the time to endorse this book; you are much appreciated. To our commissioning editor, Alec and production manager, Supraja, your professionalism is unparalleled. You made the process seamless.

Finally, to our readers, thank you for your interest and engagement. It is our hope that this book will not only provide valuable insights but also inspire further discussion and innovation in responsible use of generative AI for teaching and learning in higher education. This book is as much yours as it is ours.

Praise for *Generative AI in Higher Education*

"I found the book "Generative AI in Higher Education: Innovation Strategies for Teaching and Learning" to be a pragmatic exploration of the transformative capabilities of easily accessible AI tools, such as ChatGPT, in academia. This compelling work illuminates the significant impact of AI on educators and students alike.

One of the most persuasive arguments made is that in this era, new paradigms of teaching and learning are emerging. Those who will thrive during this phase of creative disruption are not merely those who grasp the theories and practices of education but also those who can responsibly and efficiently use AI to innovate academic practices.

This crucial insight highlights the immediate need for educators and students to responsibly adopt AI technologies in their teaching and learning methodologies.

For professors, this book provides invaluable insights that promise to revolutionise their approach to teaching with more than 15 practical use cases spanning various contexts, complemented by hands-on examples. By leveraging generative AI, educators can enhance lesson planning, assessments, and grading processes, among others. This not only conserves time and effort but also elevates the quality of instruction and scholarship when used ethically.

Moreover, "Generative AI in Higher Education" equips students with the necessary knowledge and skills to responsibly apply AI in their academic endeavours. From devising personalized study plans and student-led formative assessments to interpreting course content in a more familiar language, students are shown how to responsibly utilize the full potential of AI to boost their learning outcomes and academic achievement.

This book is an essential read for anyone looking to make a significant start with generative AI in the evolving landscape of higher education. Whether you are a seasoned professor or an eager student, it will guide you to unlock the transformative power of generative AI in teaching and learning responsibly."

—Prof. Tayo Arulogun, *Vice Chancellor, Miva Open University, FCT Abuja, Nigeria*

"As a passionate advocate for transformative and socially just educational practices, I am delighted to endorse 'Generative AI in Higher Education: Innovation Strategies for Teaching and Learning.' This book meticulously examines the integration of Generative AI (GenAI) into educational systems, offering a critical perspective that resonates deeply with both post-digital theory and critical pedagogy.

From a post-digital standpoint, this book brilliantly navigates the increasingly blurred lines between digital and non-digital realms, urging us to scrutinise the cultural and social dynamics shaped by AI technologies. It challenges us to reflect on who controls these technologies and whose knowledge is prioritized, advocating for a democratisation of knowledge production that aligns with the very essence of critical pedagogy.

Seeming to embrace Paulo Freire's principles in his critical pedagogy, the book further compels us to envision AI not merely as a tool for efficiency but as a catalyst for emancipation and student agency. It encourages the use of AI to foster critical thinking, creativity, and transformative action, thus contributing to an education that is truly a practice of freedom.

This publication is therefore a crucial resource for educators, administrators, and policymakers committed to leveraging AI to enhance educational outcomes while critically addressing the ethical considerations and power dynamics involved. It sets a foundation for a future where educational technology truly serves the collective good, fostering environments that are inclusive, equitable, and reflective of our diverse societal needs.

I highly recommend this insightful and forward-thinking book to anyone invested in shaping the future of education in the age of digital transformation."

—Prof. Hossanna Twinomurinzi, *4IR Professor and Vice Dean, Research, Innovation & Internationalisation, Centre for Applied Data Science, College of Business & Economics, University of Johannesburg, South Africa*

"I would highly recommend this as an essential title for anyone teaching classes related to generative AI. The book is informative, practical, easy to read and well-written. This book makes extensive use of examples generated by Chat GPT which are both engaging and relevant to teachers, lecturers and the students they are teaching. It draws from academic and professional literature and blends these, thus producing a unique resource for those working in higher education. AI and in particular, generative AI, is rapidly becoming an important "hot" topic for computer science students. This book encapsulates current thinking and practice in this field."

—Peter Smith, *Emeritus Professor, University of Sunderland, UK*

"As a university leader whose role involves, among many other things, navigating the unfolding impact of generative artificial intelligence (AI) on higher education, I find the book "Generative AI in Higher Education: Innovation Strategies for Teaching and Learning" both relevant and timely. The authors draw on several years of research and teaching practice to offer an insightful discussion of how AI tools can be applied across various pedagogical contexts. They provide actionable strategies to enhance educational outcomes and student engagement using generative AI.

The book provides a thorough theoretical grounding but also practical examples that are immediately relevant to educators and policymakers. From enhancing lesson preparation to revolutionising assessments and personalised learning, the book addresses critical aspects of teaching and learning that are pivotal for the adaptation of higher education to the demands of the twenty-first century.

The book's balanced approach to the opportunities and ethical challenges of using generative AI is particularly commendable. It offers the necessary framework to implement AI solutions in a way that is both innovative and mindful of the broader social and educational impact.

Stakeholders in higher education, including teachers, leaders and policymakers, will find this book useful. It is indeed a must-read for those committed to embracing the digital transformation in education with a responsible and forward-thinking approach."

—Prof. David Mba, *Vice Chancellor, Birmingham City University, United Kingdom*

"The release of ChatGPT to the general public took higher education by surprise. While AI specialists had been discussing generative AI for a while, its integration into an interactive easily accessible web platform increased accessibility and use in unforeseen ways. We are still grappling with the question what the consequences of the wide availability of generative AI will be. But, looking back, it seems that higher education was among the first sectors that recognised that generative AI could be a game changer in many different ways. Among the first applications that were perceived to be likely was the use of ChatGPT by students to help them with their assignments in ways that could run counter to the intention of the assessment regime. Many universities therefore scrambled to develop policies to guide students' use of generative AI and they often did so in ways that restrict its use.

The book by Owoseni, Kolade, and Egbetokun is an important and timely contribution to this debate and it positively differs from much of the debate by exploring the opportunities and benefits that generative AI can offer. Rather than focusing on the potential of students' cheating in essays, they take a much more rounded and comprehensive approach looking at the potential of generative AI in curriculum development, different types of assessment, teaching delivery, and student engagement. They provide practical examples of how generative AI can be employed in ways that is beneficial to teachers, learners, and learning outcomes.

We don't know which changes ChatGPT will engender eventually. While we are grappling with this question, the technology itself evolves and new technologies and capabilities are emerging. The one thing we can be certain of is that technical progress promises more and ever faster change across all aspects of society. Higher education has a key role in driving but also reflecting on and governing this change. Higher education institutions therefore need to be open, receptive, but also careful and measured when engaging with new technologies. Owoseni, Kolade, and Egbetokun's book is an excellent example of a proactive and supportive approach to a technology that promises a key driver of change.

I encourage educators and other higher education staff to engage with it, reflect on the examples, and use the positive perspective to inform their own practice in teaching, research, and higher education governance."

—Professor Bernd Stahl, *Professor of Critical Research in Technology, School of Computer Science, University of Nottingham, United Kingdom*

"In an era of rapid technological advancements, the integration of Generative Artificial Intelligence (AI) into higher education is a transformative milestone. This groundbreaking book, driven by innovation, offers unique insights into the profound implications of Generative AI for both students and educators. It provides a comprehensive understanding of implications and applications for lesson preparation, content development, formative learning and assessment, responsible use, personalized learning, student engagement, and emerging issues shaping the educational landscape of tomorrow.

This book is a journey through how Generative AI can be integrated into the fabric of higher education. From the inception of lesson planning to the execution of dynamic classroom experiences, Generative AI serves as a catalyst for pedagogical innovation. It equips educators with practical tools that streamline content creation, adapt to diverse learning styles, and foster an environment conducive to deep learning. Moreover, this book illuminates the ethical dimensions of AI implementation, emphasizing the crucial role of educators as stewards of knowledge. It underscores the importance of responsible use and mindful engagement, empowering educators to navigate the ethical complexities inherent in AI.

Furthermore, Generative AI redefines the paradigm of personalized learning, tailoring educational experiences to each student's unique needs and preferences. Educators can cultivate a dynamic learning ecosystem through adaptive algorithms and real-time feedback mechanisms that promote mastery and self-efficacy. Additionally, the book illuminates the transformative potential of Generative AI in enhancing student engagement and retention. By harnessing the power of interactive simulations, immersive experiences, and gamified learning environments, educators can captivate students' hearts and minds, igniting a passion for lifelong learning.

As we navigate the ever-changing landscape of higher education, this book serves as a compass, guiding readers through the emerging issues and future considerations shaping the educational frontier. From the ethical implications of AI bias to the integration of augmented reality in the classroom, the book equips educators with the knowledge and tools needed to thrive in an era of unprecedented technological innovation. In conclusion, with its rich insights, practical strategies, and visionary outlook, this book will empower educators and students alike to understand and apply the possibilities of Generative AI in Higher Education."

—Sunday A. Leonard, *PhD, Head of Secretariat, Scientific and Technical Advisory Panel to the Global Environment Facility, United Nations Environment Programme, Washington DC*

"I read this book through the lens of a development-oriented third sector practitioner. Since education is pivotal to development, I congratulate the authors for this work, which, though it appears sector-specific, has the distinct potential of impacting all sectors of society. They have managed to treat the subject in such a comprehensive manner that it will undoubtedly be of great benefit, not only to its primary targets, but also to a much wider audience including all progressive drivers of socio-economic public policy.

The book delves into the many advantages of Generative AI. At the same time, rather than disregard the various challenges that have been widely thought to be inherent in it, the book cleverly provides both theoretical and practical ways of containing the risks whilst conserving its vast benefits. I consider it a valuable and most enlightening addition to the emerging literature aimed at enhancing the understanding and constructive use of Generative AI by all. Including all 'students' of the future of mankind."

—Ọlatokunbọ Awolọwọ Dosumu, *Executive Director of The Obafemi Awolowo Foundation, Former Nigerian Ambassador to the Netherlands*

Contents

List of Prompts

List of Figures

List of Tables

CHAPTER 1

Generative AI and Its Implications for Higher Education Students and Educators

1.1 Introduction

Since the launch of ChatGPT by Open AI in November 2022, generative AI (GenAI) has captured public imagination and shaken up the higher education sector. With 175 trillion parameters at its command, ChatGPT4 is one of the largest and most powerful GenAI models available, with vast and versatile capabilities surpassing previous chatbot models. GenAI is especially powerful for new content creation. With simple commands, users can generate new content on a wide range of topics, across a whole spectrum of formats and styles, tailored for various audiences and platforms. For example, GenAIs such as ChatGPT have been used to compose original pieces of fiction, poetry, and even entire novels. More recently, GenAI algorithms are now being used to generate stunning images ranging from real-life mimics to abstract paintings, some of which have been featured in art galleries. GenAI is also being used to generate scripts and dialogues, and even to animate characters. News outlets are experimenting with AI to generate articles, reports, and news summaries. In marketing, brands are now deploying GenAI to generate different promotional materials, social media posts, and creative content for adverts.

Within the education sector, GenAI opportunities and possibilities are seemingly endless. GenAI is being used to create customised learning materials, interactive modules, quizzes, and other dynamic content that

A. Owoseni et al., *Generative AI in Higher Education*,
https://doi.org/10.1007/978-3-031-60179-8_1

engage and enrich the learning experience of students. This will be explored in more detail later in this chapter. For researchers, GenAI is a powerful and effective assistive tool that can be summoned to help with drafting literature reviews and grant proposal, and with grammar checking and language polishing. It can also assist with time-consuming activities like data cleaning and data visualisation, drawing on large datasets to generate graphs, charts, and tables that enhance the aesthetics and presentational value of manuscripts. In effect, GenAI can enhance researcher productivity by freeing up researchers from time-intensive tasks so they can focus more attention on the critical and creative aspects of their work, thereby enhancing overall quality and impact.

However, like most technologies, GenAI also lends itself to different sorts of abuses. In the higher education (HE) sector, abusive deployment of generative AI constitutes the ultimate nightmare scenario for HE institutions and practitioners. For a sector that has, for decades, been grappling with the perennial, seemingly intractable problem of essay mills, the emergence and rapid spread of generative AI represents an existential threat. With simple commands, students can now generate entire academic essays that can score high on originality and pass the scrutiny of most official plagiarism checks. For some practitioners, the GenAI phenomenon strikes at the heart of HE enterprise, and it should be nipped in the bud before it goes out of control. This group led the call for outright ban of GenAI when it first emerged. In time, majority of HE stakeholders have come to the realisation that resistance against a disruptive technology like GenAI is a fool's errand.

The challenge then in the sector is to find ways to mitigate the inherent risks, guard against its abuses, and find creative and innovative ways to make the best of what GenAI has to offer. Leaders in the HE sector are beginning to put together policies that would control the use of GenAI responsibly, but there is still a wide knowledge and skill gap in exploring the capabilities of GenAI for teaching and learning, which then raise the question—how can educators develop effective policies to manage the use of innovative GenAI technology without having firsthand experience with the technology themselves? Knowledge often comes through experimentation and usage. This is a major rationale for this book. It provides a practical guide on how educators can leverage GenAI. Moreover, the book sets out an agenda for responsible use of GenAI by highlighting key themes that have attracted debates and elicited important insights about the challenge and promise of GenAI in the HE sectors. The book is structured to offer prompts and content from GenAI along with screenshots, and in some cases, conceptual frameworks that exemplify responsible use of GenAI in HE.

In this introductory chapter, we begin by describing the key functionalities and operational processes of GenAI, and what they mean for the business of knowledge production and how intellectual product is, and should be, attributed. This is followed by a discussion of the challenge AI poses to learning itself. In other words, if GenAI is such a powerful tool for aggregating and synthesising knowledge, is it now more important than ever to push the frontiers of learning beyond accumulation and generation of new knowledge to application of same to solve real world and abstract problems, and demonstration of these solutions where possible and appropriate? These then feed into the next section and question of: how do we, in this rapidly changing landscape, verify and certify what learners have acquired, in terms of knowledge, competencies, and demonstrable performance? The final section offers critical reflection on the possibilities and opportunities that can be harnessed if GenAI is coopted by HE practitioners as useful tools to shake and change things up in terms of educational content, AI-enabled feedforward and feedback systems, and computer serious games that, when creatively deployed, can deeply enrich the learning experience of students and better prepare them for the twenty-first-century knowledge economy.

1.2 Knowledge Production and Attribution: How Does GenAI Work?

I just asked ChatGPT to generate an argument in favour of, and then against, the proposition that GenAI such as ChatGPT is a mere aggregator and not a true generator of knowledge, and the super chatbot is therefore unworthy of author attribution. The responses are fascinating and did creditably well to articulate the key points of debates that have caught the interest and support of scholars and stakeholders on both sides of the arguments. In an opinion piece published in the New York Times, American linguist Noam Chomsky, who some may regard as a sceptic of natural language models, argued at length that generative AIs like ChatGPT are incapable of the sort of sophisticated reasoning and knowledge production that we attribute to the human mind. Rather than create original knowledge, Chomsky says, ChatGPT relies entirely on existing and vast database created by humans in order to produce what in the end are only probabilistic responses to scientific questions:

> The human mind is not, like ChatGPT and its ilk, a lumbering statistical engine for pattern matching, gorging on hundreds of terabytes of data and extrapolating the most likely conversational response or most probable answer to a scientific question. On the contrary, the human mind is a surprisingly efficient and even elegant system that operates with small amounts of information; it seeks not to infer brute correlations among data points but to create explanations (Chomsky et al., 2023).

Chomsky goes on to say that that ChatGPT is unable to give a definitive answer to most scientific questions. It can only answer in probabilities. So, it is important, from the outset, to address the fundamental about whether generative AI is indeed a knowledge producer, and, if so, what kind of knowledge can be attributed to it. The pros and cons outputs generated by ChatGPT in Prompt 1.1 is telling a useful starting point.

Prompt 1.1: ChatGPT, knowledge aggregators or knowledge creator

Prompt

"ChatGPT is mere aggregator, not a generator, of knowledge. It should not claim attribution" Produce a 200-word argument in favour of this proposition, and another 200-word against this proposition.

ChatGPT Response

In Favor:

ChatGPT operates as an advanced aggregator of existing knowledge, meticulously sifting through vast datasets to provide responses that mirror the input it has been trained on. Its core functionality does not involve the creation of new knowledge or original insights but rather the recombination of pre-existing information in a coherent and contextually relevant manner. This process, while impressive, is fundamentally different from human cognitive abilities that generate new ideas, theories, or creative works based on original thought processes. Given this distinction, attributing authorship or originality to ChatGPT's outputs misconstrues its role in the knowledge ecosystem. It synthesizes and presents information based on patterns learned from its training data, lacking the intentionality and consciousness that underpin human creativity and intellectual contribution. Therefore, claiming attribution for its outputs could dilute the value of original thought and creativity, elements that are central to intellectual advancements and cultural developments. Recognition of ChatGPT's role should remain within the bounds of what it truly is—a highly sophisticated tool for aggregating and re-presenting existing knowledge.

Against:
Arguing that ChatGPT is merely an aggregator and not a generator of knowledge underestimates the complexity and utility of generative AI models. ChatGPT, through its advanced algorithms, does more than compile information; it processes and interacts with input in ways that can produce outputs not explicitly present in its training data. This ability to generate coherent, contextually appropriate responses in real-time conversation or problem-solving scenarios demonstrates a form of knowledge generation. It's not about creating knowledge in the academic or scientific sense but about synthesizing and applying the vast array of data it has been trained on to new, unseen questions and problems. Furthermore, attributing the work done by ChatGPT to the model itself acknowledges the sophistication of AI development and encourages further innovation in the field. While the knowledge ChatGPT works with originates from human creators, the unique combination, interpretation, and presentation of that knowledge in new contexts is a valuable process. This capability supports learning, creativity, and decision-making in ways that complement human intellect, suggesting that ChatGPT, and similar AI models, represent a new frontier in our understanding and utilization of knowledge.

ChatGPT Screen

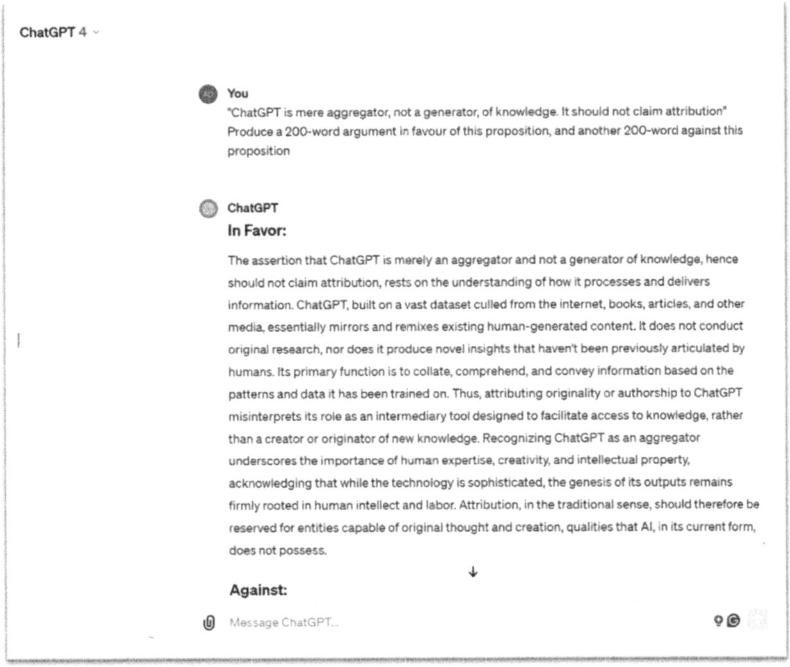

The “pros and cons” output from ChatGPT sums of the arguments about the merits and limits of generative AI. It also underlines a fundamental question that lends itself to a more nuanced answer. That is: what kind of knowledge are we talking about, in fact? ChatGPT says generative AI demonstrates “a form of knowledge generation”, but it is not knowledge in the “academic or scientific sense”. Rather, it is “knowledge” based on synthesis and analysis of a “vast array of data” to elucidate, if not resolve, new questions and problems. When pressed further, via appropriate prompts, on this distinction, ChatGPT identified four types each of human-generated knowledge and computer-generated knowledge (see Prompt 1.2).

Prompt 1.2: Exploring human and AI generated knowledge
Prompt
In short bullet points, name and describe different types of knowledge- in the context of human generated knowledge versus AI generated knowledge.

ChatGPT Response

Human-Generated Knowledge:

- *Explicit Knowledge:* Clearly articulated and codified knowledge, such as books, articles, and manuals. Humans create explicit knowledge through formal communication and documentation.
- *Tacit Knowledge:* Personal, context-specific knowledge embedded in experiences and actions, often difficult to formalize or communicate. It includes skills, ideas, and intuitions developed through human experiences.
- *Cultural Knowledge:* Collective wisdom and practices shared among a group, shaped by historical, social, and environmental factors. It encompasses traditions, languages, and norms passed through generations.
- *Creative Knowledge:* Original ideas and artistic expressions conceived through human creativity and imagination, leading to innovations, artworks, and literary works.

AI-Generated Knowledge:

- *Synthesized Knowledge:* Information generated by AI through the analysis and combination of vast datasets, producing summaries, forecasts, or recommendations based on existing data.
- *Pattern-Based Knowledge:* Knowledge derived from identifying patterns and correlations in large datasets that might not be immediately apparent to humans, useful in fields like market analysis or medical diagnosis.
- *Simulated Knowledge:* AI's ability to model and simulate complex systems or scenarios, providing insights into possible outcomes and behaviours within virtual environments.
- *Adapted Knowledge:* AI systems can learn from new data inputs to adapt responses and generate knowledge that fits emerging patterns or questions, although initially grounded in their training data.

ChatGPT Screen

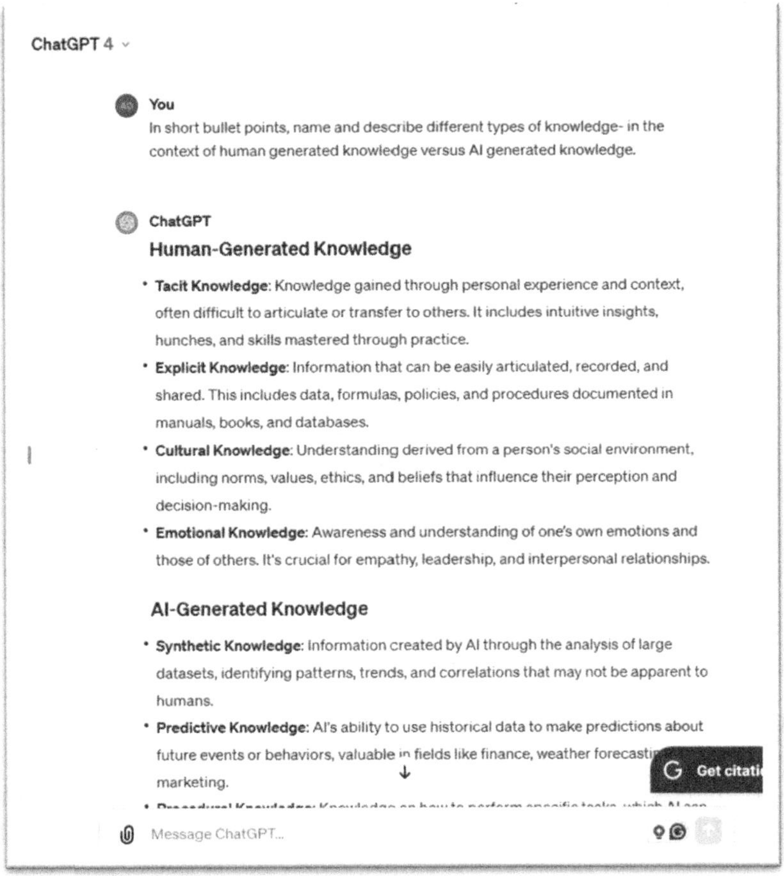
ChatGPT 4

You
In short bullet points, name and describe different types of knowledge- in the context of human generated knowledge versus AI generated knowledge.

ChatGPT
Human-Generated Knowledge

- **Tacit Knowledge:** Knowledge gained through personal experience and context, often difficult to articulate or transfer to others. It includes intuitive insights, hunches, and skills mastered through practice.
- **Explicit Knowledge:** Information that can be easily articulated, recorded, and shared. This includes data, formulas, policies, and procedures documented in manuals, books, and databases.
- **Cultural Knowledge:** Understanding derived from a person's social environment, including norms, values, ethics, and beliefs that influence their perception and decision-making.
- **Emotional Knowledge:** Awareness and understanding of one's own emotions and those of others. It's crucial for empathy, leadership, and interpersonal relationships.

AI-Generated Knowledge

- **Synthetic Knowledge:** Information created by AI through the analysis of large datasets, identifying patterns, trends, and correlations that may not be apparent to humans.
- **Predictive Knowledge:** AI's ability to use historical data to make predictions about future events or behaviors, valuable in fields like finance, weather forecasti marketing.

Get citati

Message ChatGPT...

1.3 Generative AI: Bad Enemy, Great Friend

The distinctions outlined by ChatGPT in Prompt 1.2 suggest that the question as to whether GenAI generates, rather than merely aggregates, knowledge should be framed in a nuanced manner that acknowledges and delineates the kinds of knowledge that can be attributed to generative AI models like ChatGPT. It can be argued, of course, that if these different types of knowledge were to be organised into a kind of hierarchical structure, human-generated knowledge, especially creative knowledge, will be in the upper echelons. In a similar vein, it can be argued that AI-generated knowledge is often complementary and not exclusive to human-generated knowledge. For example, the simulation of complex systems can generate useful insights that are valuable, and sometimes critical, for the creative production of new empirical knowledge.

These distinctions also raise arguably a more fundamental question about the viability and future of teaching and learning activities such as academic essays and the concomitant question as to whether higher education institutions must now revisit teaching and learning priorities in the wake of new AI capabilities. To explicate, academic essays do not typically require scientific originality in the way this is understood and measured in journal manuscripts, say. What essays require, more often than not, is language originality in presenting ideas that are generally established rather than new. The task of writing "original" essays therefore typically entails a lot of synthesis of extant knowledge and data, often to tease out new insights that are valuable but still do not qualify as new scientific knowledge. As we have noted, this is a domain in which GenAI models thrive and excel. This begs the question as to if and why universities should continue to prioritise this type of knowledge, or whether the future of learning should prioritise other types of outcomes beyond know-what. It is to this question that we now turn our attention in the next section.

1.4 Learning in the Twenty-First Century: From Know-What to Know-How and Show-How

Historically, the two principal missions of higher education have been identified as research and teaching. In recent decades, the emergence of non-university actors such as Massive Open Online Courses (MOOCs) platforms has brought increased scrutiny and pressure on universities to deliver better value for money on their offerings. Generative AI has added extra weight and urgency to this scrutiny. University teaching and learning structures are designed to not only impart knowledge but develop critical thinking that enables learners to question establish knowledge and synthesise different perspectives in order to generate new insights. In recent times, more attention is being given to the development of transferrable skills as an important learning outcome for university students. However, much of the assessment (to which we shall soon turn attention) is focused on testing students' understanding of established knowledge, and their critical thinking ability to interrogate received knowledge in order to generate new insights.

There is no doubt that understanding established knowledge is an important foundation in the learning process. Without understanding, it is practically impossible to generate new insights or produce original knowledge. However, this is where the AI challenge to the learning process begins to emerge. Understanding entails active and time-intensive application intellectual by the learner. To use an example, a learner seeking to understand the theory of planned behaviour, a well-known theory in psychology and vocational behaviour, will be expected to read not only the original article by Ajzen (1991) but also a few other conceptual and empirical articles with different perspectives on the theory. This will deepen their understanding well enough to properly critique the theory and generate new insights. However, with generative AI, a learner can bypass this time-intensive and necessary process of intellectual application and instead issue a prompt to "critique the theory of planned behaviour", as Prompt 1.3 shows.

Prompt 1.3: Critique the theory of planned behaviour

Prompt
Critique, in 200 words, the theory of planned behaviour, highlighting the strengths and weaknesses of this theory.

ChatGPT Response
The Theory of Planned Behavior (TPB) is a psychological framework that predicts individual behavior based on three key determinants: attitudes toward the behavior, subjective norms, and perceived behavioral control. A strength of TPB is its comprehensive nature, incorporating both internal attitudes and external social influences, making it applicable across a diverse range of behaviors and contexts. This inclusivity allows for a nuanced understanding of how various factors contribute to behavior intention and actual behavior, providing valuable insights for designing interventions aimed at changing behavior.

However, TPB is not without its weaknesses. One criticism is its assumption that behavior is the result of a rational decision-making process, potentially overlooking impulsive or habitual actions that occur without deliberate planning. This can limit the theory's applicability to behaviors that are less conscious or more emotionally driven. Furthermore, TPB assumes that individuals have complete volitional control over their behavior, which may not account for situations where external constraints limit an individual's ability to perform a desired behavior. Finally, the theory's focus on intention as the primary predictor of behavior may not always account for the gap between intention and action, as individuals might fail to translate their intentions into behavior due to unforeseen circumstances or changes in their situation.

ChatGPT Screen

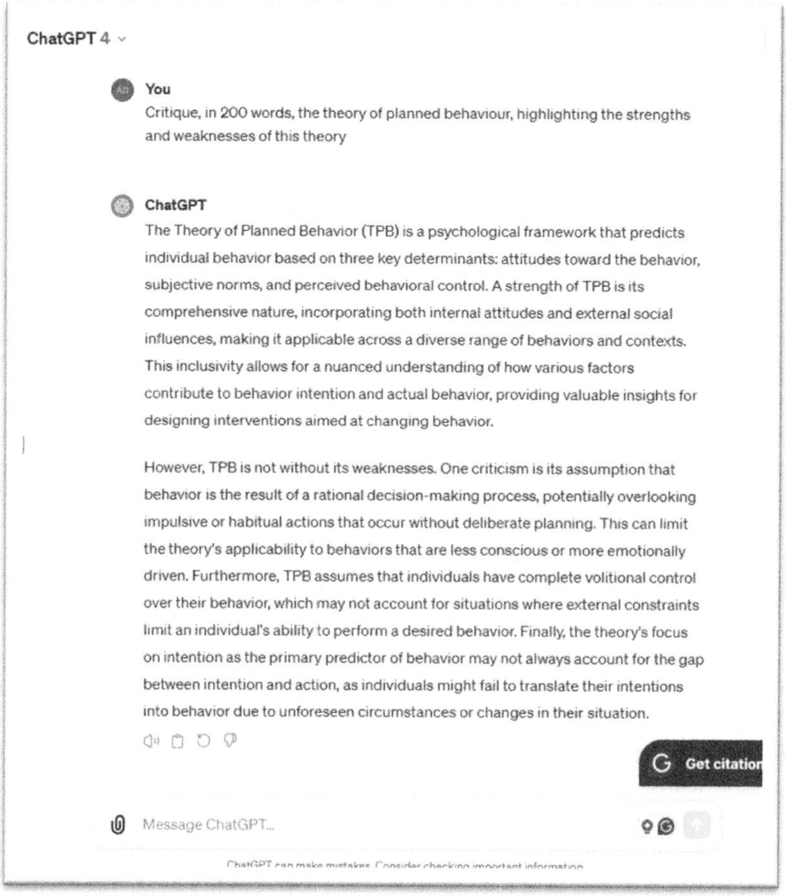

The entry above is credible enough to get a B pass, say, but it underlines the scale of the challenge to learning. If ChatGPT can produce a credible critique like this, why should a learner bother to read five to ten journal manuscripts to gain a deeper understanding, unless of course the motivation is not simply to get a pass grade but to acquire the knowledge and gain understanding? And without the incentive for a pass grade, why should a student want to acquire the knowledge, if it takes more effort and time? There is a philosophical response to this question which cannot be discussed at full length here because of the limitation of scope and space but still important to highlight. It is this: knowledge is inherently valuable and necessary for the full development of the human person, enabling individuals for the Socratic pursuit of the examined life. More specifically, scholarly knowledge lays the foundation for innovation and also essential informed, evidenced decision-making at all levels. It is therefore critically important for society and to be desired and valued in and of itself. There is also a compelling practical argument to the effect that understanding concepts and ideas is a precondition to the ability to apply such concepts and ideas to a wide range of real-time problems and situations. The deeper the understanding, the better the learner is able to creatively apply them to different situations, in the process not only deepening the understanding of existing knowledge but also creating new knowledge both in abstract forms and in various contexts of applications. This argument aligns with the other one that highlight scholarly knowledge as a precursor and driver of innovation. To sum it up, knowledge is valuable not only philosophically because of what it is, but also practically because of what it can lead to: new knowledge, and applications in contexts.

The question now is, how in practice can universities incentivise students to deep learning in the age of generative AI? In our recent paper (Kolade, Owoseni & Egbetokun, 2024), we highlighted the need for a dynamic teaching and learning pedagogy that capacitates graduates for lifelong learning in a rapidly changing labour market:

> The emergence of the new knowledge economy and ongoing rapid changes precipitated by digital transformation, has heightened interest and sharpened the focus on the imperative of innovative pedagogy that prepares learners not only for the current state of the labour market but also capacitates them to adapt to changes and respond to opportunities in a rapidly evolving global economy (Kolade, Owoseni & Egbetokun, 2024, p. 12).

Learning should therefore not focus simply on knowledge acquisition (know-what) at the base of the pyramid, but also prioritise development of competencies (know-how) and demonstration of performance (show-how). A pedagogical approach that focuses the minds of learners not only on the inherent value of knowledge, but its application potentials is more likely to incentivise learners to deep learning, in spite of shortcuts presented by GenAI models. The iterative, mutually reinforcing process of learning and application deepens understanding and open new windows of applications, in the same breadth. In this process, GenAI can be co-opted by learners, not as a shortcut but as an assistive tool that helps them to streamline their intellectual application while offering unlimited feedback and new, exciting ways to access knowledge.

Learning in very specific context of applications also exposes the limitations of GenAIs in their current form. Consider the example described in Prompt 1.4 and Prompt 1.5. In the first iteration (Prompt 1.4), ChatGPT was asked to analyse, in 300 words, the growth strategy of Burendo, a high-performing SME in the Yorkshire region of England, UK. The response is made of generic paragraphs that effectively assume, but did not specify, Burendo's real-time data. These assumptions and weaknesses came clearer to light in the second prompt, which was worded more specifically to indicate that the output should draw on real-time data and not on generic assumptions. The response there was telling: "I don't have the ability to access or retrieve real-time data, including specific company performance data such as that for Burendo or any other entity as of 2023 or any other time". This raises immediate questions and ideas for the future of assessment, which we shall consider in the next section. What seems clear for now is that when real-time application is prioritised, a learner has to do much more than simply use prompt to aggregate or synthesise knowledge. They will need to invest more time to engage deeper and wider with materials in order to be able to apply the knowledge in the contexts of application. In such circumstance, banning AI is needless and probably counter-productive, to the extent that contents generated by AI can help them deepen the understanding necessary for confident application of knowledge in context.

Prompt 1.4: Analyse the growth strategy of Burendo - Task1

Prompt

Burendo is one of the top performing companies in Yorkshire, England, as of year 2023. Based on recent performance data of Burendo, identify one key strategy among many that drove its excellent growth. Keep your response to 300 words maximum.

ChatGPT Response

As of my last update in April 2023, I don't have access to real-time databases or the ability to pull new data, which includes the most recent performance data of specific companies such as Burendo. Therefore, I can't provide the latest information or insights into Burendo's performance or strategies directly. However, I can suggest a general approach to identifying a key strategy that might drive excellent growth for a top-performing company like Burendo, based on common strategies used by successful companies.

A key strategy often employed by thriving companies involves innovation and digital transformation. This strategy encompasses the integration of advanced digital technologies into all areas of a business, fundamentally changing how the company operates and delivers value to customers. For a company like Burendo, which operates in a dynamic environment, embracing digital transformation could streamline operations, enhance customer experiences, and open new markets or revenue streams. This might include adopting cloud computing, data analytics to gain insights into customer behavior, or implementing AI and machine learning for improved decision-making and efficiency.

Innovation extends beyond technology; it also involves developing new business models, pioneering in uncharted market segments, or offering unique products or services that meet emerging customer needs. Burendo's commitment to continuous innovation could be a critical driver of its growth, setting it apart from competitors and establishing it as a leader in its industry.

Moreover, such a strategy likely supports Burendo in creating a resilient and adaptable business capable of navigating the complexities of modern markets, leveraging opportunities for expansion, and responding proactively to challenges.

ChatGPT Screen

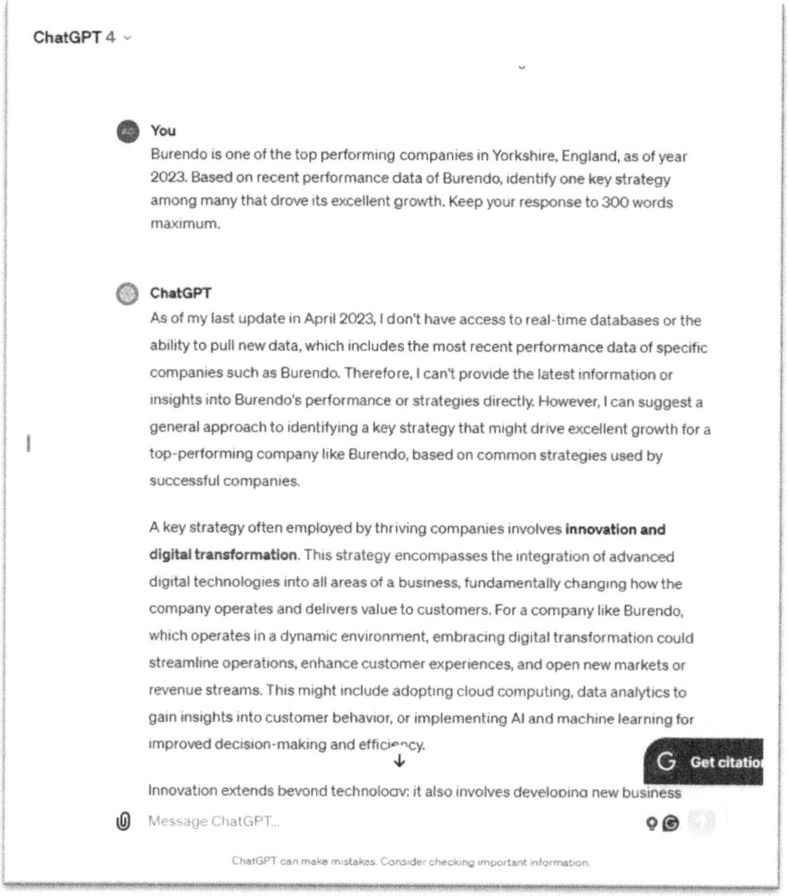

Prompt 1.5: Analyse the growth strategy of Burendo - Task2

Prompt

Burendo is one of the top performing companies in Yorkshire, England, as of year 2023. Make explicit reference to specific and recent performance data from Burendo to identify one key strategy among many that drove its excellent growth. Keep your response to 300 words maximum.

ChatGPT Response

Without real-time access to specific company data or updates beyond my last training cut-off in April 2023, I can't provide recent performance data or directly reference specific strategies employed by Burendo in Yorkshire, England. However, I can outline a hypothetical approach that a top-performing company like Burendo might employ to drive excellent growth, based on strategies common among successful businesses.

Assuming Burendo operates within a sector where customer-centric innovation is key, a strategy that could significantly contribute to its growth is the focus on developing personalized solutions tailored to meet the evolving needs of its customers. This approach involves leveraging advanced data analytics to understand customer preferences, behaviors, and feedback, thereby creating products or services that precisely cater to the target market's demands.

For instance, Burendo might have invested in R&D to innovate its product lineup or service offerings, ensuring they are not only of high quality but also incorporate features or technologies that set them apart in the marketplace. Simultaneously, enhancing the customer experience through digital platforms could make interactions with the company more seamless, improving customer satisfaction and loyalty.

Additionally, strategic partnerships with other leading firms or technology providers could have been crucial, enabling Burendo to access new technologies, markets, or distribution channels more effectively than competitors.

While this response cannot specify Burendo's actual strategies or performance data, companies that achieve significant growth often do so by combining innovative product development, exceptional customer experience, and smart partnerships, all underpinned by a strong organizational culture that embraces change and continuous improvement.

ChatGPT Screen

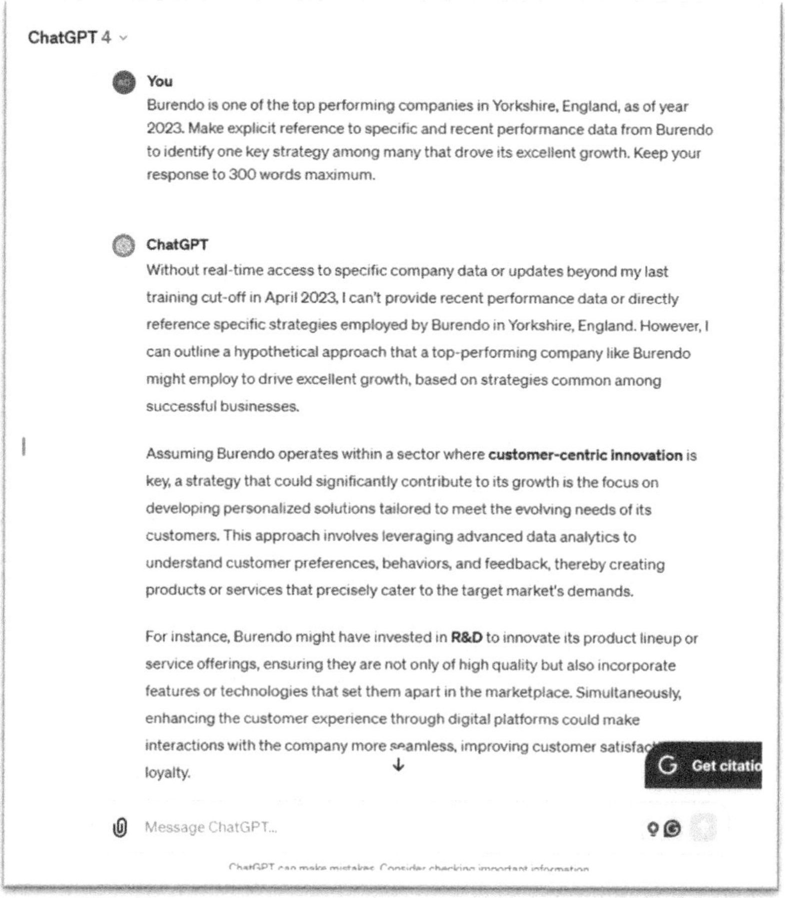

1.5 Assessments on Trial: A Question of Verification and Certification

We now turn attention to the subject of assessment. In the light of the discussion in the preceding section on teaching and learning, what assessment forms and modes will be suitable to verify and certify learning in the age of generative AI? We must begin by discussing the future of academic essays as a viable mode of assessment, given its historic popularity and now unprecedented scrutiny it has come under. This discussion is also invariably linked to the earlier points raised to distinguish between human-generated and AI-generated knowledge. As we established, generative AI is able to aggregate existing knowledge and synthesise them to generate new insights. As we have also shown in Prompt 1.4, ChatGPT was able to, not only aggregate existing knowledge but also critique them creditably for pass grade output. A note of caution is due at this point to the effect that the specific example in Prompt 1.4, of the well-known theory of planned behaviour is probably not representative. In other words, as generative AI pull resources from the good, the bad and ugly content on the web, it is prone to error and bogus content in its outputs that are not immediately evident in Prompt 1.4. Nevertheless, the overarching point is that, given enough resources and a good probability of accessing credible contents, ChatGPT was able to generate outputs with good critical content that synthesises alternative perspectives. The problem is that, often, this critique of extant knowledge and the synthesis of new insights is typically an acceptable standard expected from undergraduate essays. In other words, most undergraduate essays for module assessment (distinct from final year projects) do not require the production of original knowledge in the scientific sense of new empirical or new theoretical contribution. Instead, students are expected to demonstrate their understanding by critiquing extant knowledge and synthesising new insights—two things we have now shown that generative AI can do creditably, although not perfectly, enough to pass. If students are required, as is now the case, to prepare and submit their essays remotely, many will likely opt to use AI to generate the essays without rigorous intellectual application that is expected of them.

So, what needs to change about undergraduate, and by and large postgraduate taught, essays in the age of generative AI? Firstly, academic essays have to ask more than critique of established knowledge or synthesis of new insights from them. Educators need to inject more specific applied content into essay questions, like the Burendo example shows (Prompt 1.4, and Prompt 1.5). Such applied questions can motivate students to spend time engaging with relevant materials to deepen their understanding. Even with this, a strong case must now be made for a rethink of remote preparation of essay submission, undertaken without any controls such as browser lockdown and remote proctoring tools. Aside from being decidedly environment-unfriendly, paper exams are unwieldy to manage, both physically and administratively. They require inordinate amount of staff time. Nevertheless, electronic essays written in a controlled environment where students have no access to ChatGPT is a viable option that lends itself to additional technological applications for efficient administration of assessment. For example, remote proctoring tools, which are increasing employed by professional bodies, can be used to monitor students' activity through video, screen sharing, and AI monitoring of suspicious behaviour. In addition, browser lockdown systems can be used to prevent students from accessing other websites or applications when they are submitting an essay or writing an exam in real time. Furthermore, AI can be used to train algorithms for automated grading of written exams, building on existing technologies for automated essay scoring. This can be used to mark written essays in real time, with human assessors only required to moderate where and if necessary. Not only is this more effective than the current method, it is also more efficient.

The next question is: how do you verify and certify know-how and show-how? Universities have extensive experience in testing knowledge, and the framework of assessment is fairly straightforward. Assessment of competence (know-how) and performance (show-how) can be less straightforward. The next chapters in this book will discuss this in more detail, but it suffices here to point artificial intelligence, in one breadth a nightmare for university educators, can be the one great ally higher education providers can co-opt to enliven and enrich assessment of know-how and show-how. Artificial Intelligence (AI) is revolutionising how higher education (HE) assesses applied knowledge. Traditional work-based learning experiences like internships are valuable but often limited by resources and unequal access. AI can overcome these barriers by creating realistic simulations through serious gaming, allowing students to practise and adapt their skills to ever-changing scenarios (Ormeño et al, 2019). This not only prepares them for a dynamic twenty-first-century workplace but also fosters lifelong learning habits by enabling them to refine their competencies in a controlled, yet dynamic educational setting

(Kolade, Owoseni & Egbetokun, 2024). Formative serious games create a loop of constant learning by providing endless chances for feedback, while summative games assess learning through hands-on doing and deep immersion in the gameplay (Hainey et al, 2022). Together, these gaming experiences are crucial, allowing learners to continually gain new knowledge and adjust their skills to meet the ever-evolving demands of today's workplace (Girard et al, 2013). The facility for unlimited feedback does not replace the need for human tutor contact but frees up time for tutors to focus on higher-order teaching activities like facilitating discussions and conducting in-depth seminars.

In a sign that technology can help solve the problem technology creates, AI serious games can be designed in such a way to prevent cheating, including the use of tools like ChatGPT. This can be achieved in a number of ways. The first is dynamic content generation, that is, the process by which AI generates unique contents for each user according to their individual experience and ability level. This not only helps to mediate differentiated learning but also makes it difficult to share answers. Secondly, AI serious games typically include features for real-time monitoring of students' in-game actions and sudden changes in behaviour, including the use of terminologies not yet covered within the game's scope. Thirdly, AI serious games can incorporate adaptive difficulty, such that students who appear to be progressing too quickly can be assigned more complex challenges that require deeper understanding. Fourthly, AI serious games can be set with time limits for answering questions or making decisions. This ensures that gamers have little to no time to consult other sources, including ChatGPT, before making decisions. Finally, serious games can be built with reflective and open-ended questions that encourage critical thinking and deeper understanding.

1.6 Structure of the Book

So far, this chapter introduces the overarching aim of the book, in the wake of heightened public interest and the excitement and then consternation, among higher education practitioners, that followed the launch of ChatGPT in November 2022 by OpenAI, and subsequent unveiling of Gemini and LLaMa as competitors. The chapter provides an overview of the emergence of GenAI, exemplified by state-of-the-art generative pre-trained transformers 4 (GPT-4), built with vast and versatile capabilities that surpass previous models of chatbots. The chapter then discusses the disruptive impacts of generative AI in the higher education sector, with highlights of current debates regarding potential challenges and opportunities for learners and tutors, including raging debates about the future of academic essays. This sets the ground for the next five chapters, in which 20 use cases of GenAI are presented and discussed across a whole spectrum of themes, including lesson preparation and content development, formative assessment, summative assessment, student experience, and ethical issues. The chapter also describes the structure for the use cases chapters, including practical discussions of prompts in textboxes, hands-on tasks and exercises.

In Chapter 2, we present four use cases of GenAI in the preparation of teaching and learning materials. These cases illustrate the diverse ways in which tools like ChatGPT can support lesson preparation and content generation. Foremost, GenAI's ability to streamline teaching processes proves invaluable. By harnessing its advanced AI capabilities, educators can significantly reduce the time and effort spent on tasks such as researching, curating, and organising course materials. GenAI can quickly gather relevant information, provide comprehensive explanations, and offer practical examples, thereby facilitating efficient lesson preparation. This efficiency allows instructors to better allocate their time and resources towards other critical aspects of teaching.

Although debates persist regarding the quality and consistency of AI-generated content, this chapter aims to present evidence to inform such discussions. The use cases explored include:

- Creating a lesson plan and a pre-session checklist,
- Generating ideas and sources for asynchronous learning materials,
- Creating interactive exercises and examples, and
- Clarifying concepts.

Chapter 3 focuses on formative assessment, as it plays a pivotal role in higher education by providing ongoing feedback to both educators and students. This allows for timely adjustments to teaching and learning strategies. The real-time feedback fosters a deeper understanding of students' strengths and weaknesses, promoting active engagement and personalised learning experiences.

In simpler terms, formative assessments involve an ongoing, interactive process where learning activities and outcomes are shaped through active dialogue. Learners are actively engaged in identifying what works, areas that require improvement, and how enhancements can be made to provide a better learning experience for students.

GenAI can be applied in formative assessments through the use cases that we explored further in the chapter:

- Prompts that generate multiple-choice quizzes for webinars in a gamified approach,
- Development of scenario-based questions for small group tasks,
- Practical questions for plenary discussions, and
- Adaptive tutoring through real-time conversations and tailored content.

On the other hand, effective summative assessments should transcend mere tests of learners' ability to recall information, focusing instead on evaluating their application of knowledge. Chapter 4 explores how GenAI, including tools such as ChatGPT, can provide valuable support in various aspects of summative assessment. Firstly, these tools can assist in generating ideas for diverse types of assessments and questions. Leveraging their extensive knowledge bases and language generation capabilities, they can offer educators a variety of formats, including case studies, problem-solving tasks, and project-based assignments. This not only broadens the spectrum of assessment options but also promotes a more comprehensive evaluation of learners' abilities.

Secondly, GenAI can aid in the creation of assessment rubrics and marking guides, helping educators develop clear, comprehensive criteria for evaluating student performance. This guidance on rubric development ensures consistency in grading standards and promotes fair and objective assessments. Moreover, generative AI tools can be utilised to create sample feedback responses. These can highlight strengths, pinpoint areas for improvement, and offer suggestions for further development, thereby aiding educators in providing consistent and constructive feedback that supports student learning and growth.

It is essential to acknowledge that while GenAI offers significant advantages in summative assessment, its responsible use is imperative. Educators must be mindful of the ethical implications and ensure that AI's application aligns with the intended purposes of assessment. The chapter further explored the following use cases:

- Generating ideas for assessment types and questions,
- Creating an assessment rubric and marking guide,
- Mapping assessments to learning outcomes, and
- Creating feedback samples.

Chapter 5 addresses how educators can enhance personalised learning and student engagement through the use of GenAI. In the rapidly evolving educational landscape, personalised learning has become a pivotal approach to meet the unique needs and preferences of each student. By tailoring education to individual students' strengths, needs, skills, and interests, personalised learning significantly improves the educational experience. GenAI tools such as ChatGPT are pushing the boundaries of what's possible in personalised learning. They provide educators with a broad array of innovative tools to craft customised learning experiences that foster deeper student engagement and better knowledge retention. With the support of GenAI, educators can effectively accommodate various learning styles and paces, transforming traditional classrooms into dynamic, student-centred environments. By leveraging the diverse capabilities of generative AI, personalised learning becomes not only more feasible but also more impactful, enabling educators to design customised learning paths that optimise student engagement, knowledge retention, and overall academic achievement.

Chapter 5 explores the following use cases, demonstrating how generative AI tools can offer invaluable assistance in creating personalised learning experiences:

- Creating personalised study plans for learners,
- Developing interactive learning (serious) games tailored to learners' needs,
- Utilising ChatGPT as an intelligent and personalised tutoring assistant, and
- Generating flexible, language-specific learning content.

Chapter 6 focuses on the responsible use of GenAI by educators and students in higher education institutions (HEIs). It examines the ethical implications of employing tools like ChatGPT and proposes methods to tackle these concerns. The chapter explores use cases that raise issues about the responsible application of generative AI, including academic integrity, misinformation, bias and fairness, and proper attribution.

To confront these challenges, it is imperative for educators to adopt a conscientious approach to using GenAI. This encompasses establishing explicit guidelines for the use of GenAI tools, ensuring students comprehend their limitations, and advocating for academic integrity. Furthermore, educators are tasked with ensuring that GenAI tools are used in an inclusive and culturally sensitive manner, alongside providing instructions on how to verify information and accurately attribute content.

The main topics discussed in this chapter, accompanied by case studies, include:

- Academic integrity: highlighting the risks associated with deploying GenAI for teaching in HEIs,
- Ethics and responsibility of GenAI: two sides of the same coin,
- Towards the responsible use of GenAI in HEIs: strategies for ethical application, and
- How to use GenAI responsibly through responsible innovation framework.

The concluding Chapter 7 explores emergent issues and future considerations. It provides a summary of the main themes covered throughout the book, alongside offering forward-looking perspectives. Teaching and learning in an era dominated by GenAI differ significantly from traditional methods, impacting the required skills for both teachers and learners. Similarly, the world of work is undergoing transformations, partly driven by AI applications. This raises pivotal questions: What should the teacher and learner of the future embody? Additionally, how must the education system evolve to deliver meaningful experiences to learners and adequately prepare them for the evolving workplace? From a normative standpoint, this chapter also examines the symbiotic relationship between the productivity of Generative AI tools and their users.

References

Ajzen, I. (1991). The theory of planned behavior. *Organizational Behavior and Human Decision Processes, 50*, 179–211.

Chomsky, N., Roberts, I., & Watumull, J. (2023). *The false promise of ChatGPT*. New York Times. Guest Opinion. Available at: https://www.nytimes.com/2023/03/08/opinion/noam-chomsky-chatgpt-ai.html. Page accessed on 31-01-2024.

Girard, C., Ecalle, J., & Magnan, A. (2013). Serious games as new educational tools: How effective are they? A meta-analysis of recent studies. *Journal of Computer Assisted Learning, 29*(3), 207–219. https://doi.org/10.1111/j.1365-2729.2012.00489.x

Hainey, T., Baxter, G., Black, J., Yorke, K., Bernikas, J., Chrzanowska, N., & McAulay, F. (2022). Serious games as innovative formative assessment tools for programming in higher education. In *Proceedings of the 16th European conference on games based learning* (pp. 1–10).

Kolade, O., Owoseni, A., & Egbetokun, A. (2024). Is AI changing learning and assessment as we know it? Evidence from a ChatGPT experiment and a conceptual framework. *Heliyon, 10*(4), 1.

Ormeño, E., et al. (2019). Towards a formative instrument to evaluate user experience in virtual reality serious games. In *ACM international conference proceeding series* (pp. 53–57). Association for Computing Machinery. Available at: https://doi.org/10.1145/3364138.3364152

CHAPTER 2

Applications of Generative AI in Lesson Preparation and Content Development

2.1 Introduction

One of the main aims of formal education is to impart the knowledge and skills that prepare learners for the world of work and life in general. For this purpose, the education sector has devised a time-tested tool—structured lessons. These lessons, meticulously crafted by educators, serve as the backbone of pedagogical strategies, aiming to distill vast bodies of knowledge into digestible, engaging, and relevant learning experiences. Historically, a structured lesson will take place in a physical classroom setting. However, since the COVID-19 pandemic, virtual classrooms have become a stable component of the teaching and learning environment. In contrast to the earlier days when educators interacted with learners only within physical spaces, today's educators must adapt their preparation and content to both physical and online environments or a hybrid of both environments.

As the world undergoes rapid technological advancements, the education sector has come to a crossroads. This is facilitated by changing social landscape and digital technologies such as Generative AI (GenAI). Tools such as ChatGPT, with its capacity to generate text, images, and simulations, offer a unique opportunity for educators to customise and enrich educational materials for a wide range of scenarios. This technology not only automates certain aspects of lesson preparation but also introduces novel approaches to content generation, making education more

A. Owoseni et al., *Generative AI in Higher Education*,
https://doi.org/10.1007/978-3-031-60179-8_2

adaptable, inclusive, and aligned with the demands of the twenty-first century.

There seems to be a perpetual trade-off between the continuous search for innovative preparation and delivery methodologies and ensuring that teaching is effective and accessible. One way in which this trade-off manifests itself is the division between routine tasks and specialised ones. The distinction between routine and specialty is crucial in understanding the role of GenAI in education. It helps to highlight the potential of GenAI tools to streamline processes and enhance pedagogical strategies. Table 2.1 illustrates the division between routine tasks that can be streamlined or automated through the use of GenAI tools and those that require the nuanced judgement, empathy, and expertise of human educators. While GenAI can significantly reduce the time educators spend on administrative and preparatory tasks, the specialised tasks underscore the irreplaceable value of the educator's role in fostering a rich, interactive, and personalised learning experience.

Table 2.1 Examples of routine and specialised tasks in education

Routine tasks	*Specialised tasks*
Creating lesson plans	Adapting teaching strategies to individual learning styles
Generating quizzes and exams	Providing in-depth, personalised feedback
Marking assignments and tests	Fostering critical thinking and creativity
Managing classroom resources	Developing and implementing inclusive teaching practices
Organising student data and performance records	Mentoring and counselling students
Summarising educational content	Engaging with ethical and moral reasoning in content delivery
Generating standard communication with parents	Facilitating complex discussions and debates
Automating attendance records	Designing and leading project-based learning
Producing generic instructional materials	Assessing and integrating emerging technologies into the curriculum
Scheduling classes and allocating resources	Cultivating a positive and supportive classroom environment

Source ChatGPT 4.0. Prompt: "Can you give me a table of routine and specialized tasks in education? Use British spelling" (04/02/2024, 8.33am GMT)

Routine tasks in education often encompass the preparatory and administrative duties that, while essential, can consume a huge portion of educators' time. These include creating lesson plans, generating quizzes and exams, marking assignments, and managing classroom resources. GenAI can revolutionise these tasks by automating the creation of customised learning materials based on specific curriculum goals or student needs. For instance, GenAI algorithms can swiftly generate a variety of test questions tailored to the learning objectives of a particular lesson or produce summaries and notes that can help students grasp complex concepts more easily. This automation not only increases efficiency but also allows educators to devote more time to engaging directly with students, thus enhancing the learning experience.

On the other hand, specialised tasks in education involve complex decision-making, personalised instruction, and the nuanced understanding of student behaviour and needs—areas where the human touch is irreplaceable. These tasks include providing in-depth feedback on student work, adapting teaching strategies to accommodate diverse learning styles, and fostering critical thinking and creativity through interactive discussions and projects. While GenAI can support these endeavours by offering data-driven insights and recommendations, the role of educators remains central. For example, GenAI-generated analytics can help teachers identify patterns in student performance, enabling targeted interventions for those who may need extra support. Furthermore, GenAI can facilitate the creation of dynamic, simulation-based learning environments that encourage exploratory learning and real-world problem-solving, yet it is the educator who guides, interprets, and contextualises these experiences for their students.

A direct implication of the above is that education today needs to synthesise the capabilities of GenAI with the expertise of educators. This is arguably the only way to navigate the trade-off between innovation and effectiveness. By automating routine tasks, GenAI frees educators to focus on the specialised tasks that demand their unique skills and insights. This collaborative approach not only optimises educational outcomes but also ensures that teaching remains both effective and deeply human-centred. Through this lens, the future of education appears not as a battleground between technology and tradition, but as a fertile ground for synergy, where the goal of preparing learners for the challenges and opportunities of the future can be achieved more creatively and efficiently. The rest of this chapter illustrates how the most popular GenAI tools—ChatGPT and

Gemini (formerly Bard)—could be applied to support routine tasks in a way that leaves room for innovative pedagogy. The focus of the chapter is on lesson preparation and content development.

2.2 The Context: Using GenAI for Lesson Preparation

To create a context, we shall consider the setting of a postgraduate level course on entrepreneurship. It should be noted that this is an example for illustration purposes only. The illustrated actions and steps may be extrapolated across different contexts. Our purpose here is to exemplify how ChatGPT could be used to augment the lecturer's skills in creating an impactful learning experience for the learners. Admittedly, different individual lecturers will prepare in their own specific way; thus, the use cases included in this chapter are not meant to be replicated verbatim but to serve not just as a guide but also as a source of inspiration for individualised applications. The context under consideration is that of a lecturer who would like to explore the use of ChatGPT for developing a postgraduate level course on entrepreneurship. To make a start, it could be useful to reflect on the steps to follow. To do this, the lecturer might prompt ChatGPT as illustrated in Prompt 2.1. The exact prompt, "What are the main steps to prepare for teaching a postgraduate course on entrepreneurship?" Like an expert instructor, ChatGPT recommends following a structured approach that begins with defining learning outcomes and developing a curriculum. In practice, other activities like pre-teaching checklists, lesson plans, class activities, short cases, and proofreading will also be included.[1] The approach also includes overarching considerations such as feedback and continuous professional development which are relevant not only to the course at hand but to the teaching professional's overall practice. It is evident from Prompt 2.1 that despite the phenomenal capabilities of ChatGPT, it is not a replacement for the professional. Also, the focus on the concept of entrepreneurship is broad; ChatGPT may be able to generate more relatable ideas if the scope is narrowed to, for instance, social entrepreneurship.

[1] Some more complex tasks such as creating draft slideshows are possible with ChatGPT-4 but we will leave that to the curious reader to explore.

Prompt 2.1: Idea for creating a course on the subject of "Entrepreneurship"

Prompt

What are the main steps to prepare for teaching a postgraduate course on entrepreneurship?

ChatGPT Response

Preparing to teach a postgraduate course on entrepreneurship involves a series of thoughtful steps aimed at creating an engaging, informative, and practical learning experience for students. Here's a structured approach to designing and delivering a course in this dynamic field:

1. Define Course Objectives and Learning Outcomes
    - *Identify Key Competencies:* Determine the essential skills, knowledge, and attitudes students should develop, such as business planning, innovation management, and risk assessment.
    - *Learning Outcomes:* Clearly articulate what students are expected to know, understand, and be able to do by the end of the course.
2. Develop a Syllabus
    - *Course Content:* Outline the topics and subtopics to be covered, ensuring they align with the learning outcomes.
    - *Readings and Resources:* Select textbooks, articles, case studies, and other resources that provide theoretical knowledge and practical insights into entrepreneurship.
    - *Assessment Methods*: Design assessments that evaluate students' understanding, critical thinking, and application of entrepreneurial concepts (e.g., business plans, pitch presentations, reflective essays).
3. Incorporate Practical Experiences
    - *Guest Speakers:* Invite entrepreneurs and industry experts to share their experiences, challenges, and successes.
    - *Case Studies:* Use real-world cases to discuss strategic decision-making, problem-solving, and the implications of various actions.

- *Project-Based Learning:* Encourage students to develop their own entrepreneurial projects, fostering practical skills and innovative thinking.

4. Leverage Technology and Tools
   - *Learning Management System (LMS):* Utilize an LMS for distributing materials, facilitating discussions, and managing submissions.
   - *Digital Tools:* Integrate tools for business modeling, financial analysis, and market research to enhance students' technical skills.
5. Create an Engaging Learning Environment
   - *Interactive Methods:* Employ discussions, debates, and workshops to encourage active participation and critical thinking.
   - *Support Diversity:* Recognize and value diverse perspectives, ensuring inclusivity in the learning environment.
6. Plan for Continuous Feedback and Improvement
   - *Feedback Mechanisms:* Implement regular feedback opportunities (e.g., surveys, open discussions) to understand students' experiences and adjust teaching strategies accordingly.
   - *Reflect on Practice:* Continuously reflect on teaching effectiveness and student engagement to identify areas for enhancement.
7. Stay Updated
   - *Continuous Learning:* Keep abreast of the latest trends, research, and practices in entrepreneurship to ensure the course remains relevant and impactful.
   - *Professional Development:* Engage in workshops, conferences, and other opportunities to refine teaching methods and deepen subject matter expertise.
8. Logistical Preparation
   - *Course Schedule:* Organize the timeline of sessions, ensuring a logical flow and adequate time for each topic.

- *Room and Equipment:* Confirm classroom arrangements and ensure access to necessary equipment (e.g., projectors, internet access).

By following these steps, you can design a comprehensive and engaging postgraduate course on entrepreneurship that equips students with the knowledge, skills, and mindset to navigate the complexities of starting and growing businesses.

ChatGPT Screen

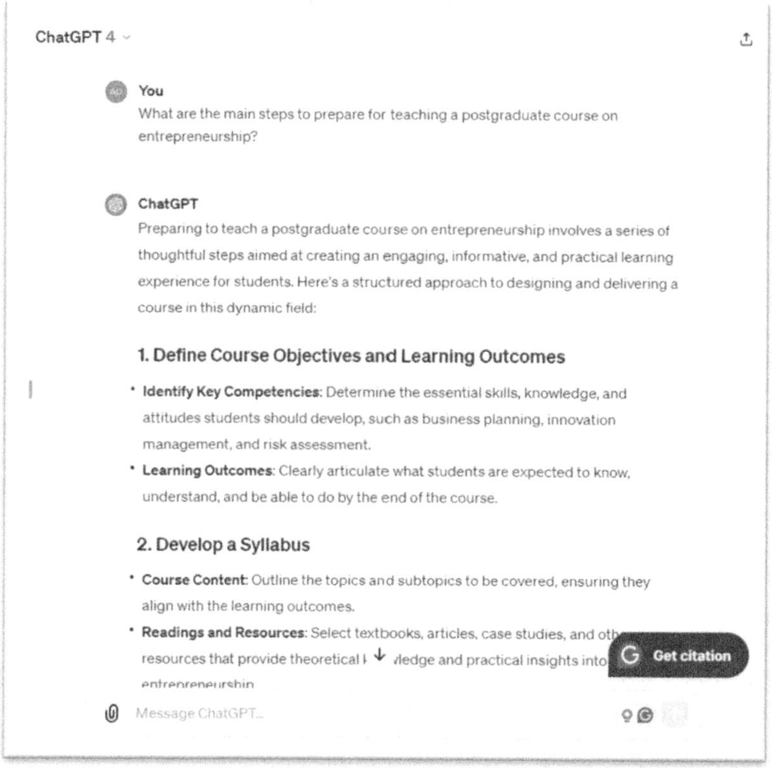

2.3 Case 1: Curriculum Development

With reference to the context outlined above, the first task is to define the curriculum that will guide the direction and content of the course that is being developed. This is particularly relevant in today's rapidly changing environment where the half-life of knowledge is short. In this sense, it is critical to ensure dynamic interaction between education administrators who set the agenda and the practitioners who implement this agenda. For instance, in some learning environments the curriculum is pre-defined by the institution whereas, in others, the teacher decides what is taught. In either situation, effective education will ensure that the interest of the learner is at the centre of curriculum development. This process can be facilitated with GenAI tools. Prompt 2.2 provides an illustration of how this may be done. In this case, ChatGPT is instructed to generate learning objectives and curriculum for the entrepreneurship course. To ensure relevance, the prompt provides some contextual information, including some demographic information about the students and their level of study.

The output detailed in Prompt 2.2 could be taken as starting material for the course curriculum. Three things are worth noting about this output. First, the curriculum matches well with the learning objectives, similar to what the human teacher will generate from scratch. By starting with ChatGPT, therefore, the teacher will save a sizeable amount of time. Secondly, the suggested topics are broad and shallow, highlighting the need for the expertise and skills of the human teacher who will refine the content. Thirdly, the use of keywords like understand, develop, and evaluate in the learning objectives is similar to what is expected in standard learning outcomes like the widely used Bloom's taxonomy (Bloom et al, 1956).

Prompt 2.2: Curriculum development using ChatGPT

Prompt

Consider that the student cohort comprises a highly international group of master's degree students from various countries, including the UK, Nigeria, India, Pakistan, South Africa, and the United States. Generate 3 learning objectives for the course and create a detailed curriculum for a 6-week duration. Explore the use of a wide range of teaching approaches.

ChatGPT Response

Given the diverse and international nature of the student cohort, the course should be designed to not only provide robust content on entrepreneurship but also to cultivate a global perspective, foster intercultural competence, and leverage the rich backgrounds of the students. Here are three learning objectives, followed by a detailed 6-week curriculum that employs various teaching approaches.

Learning Objectives:

- *Understand Global Entrepreneurial Ecosystems:* Students will gain insights into how different cultural, economic, and regulatory environments affect entrepreneurial ventures across countries including the UK, Nigeria, India, Pakistan, South Africa, and the United States.
- *Develop Critical Thinking and Innovation Skills:* Through the analysis of case studies, creation of business models, and problem-solving exercises, students will learn to apply innovative thinking and strategic analysis in diverse business scenarios.
- Cultivate Cross-Cultural Communication and Leadership Skills: Engaging in group projects and discussions, students will enhance their abilities to communicate effectively, negotiate, and lead in multicultural and multidisciplinary teams.

6-Week Curriculum Overview:

- *Week 1:* Introduction to Global Entrepreneurship
    - Lecture: Overview of entrepreneurship and its significance in various economies.
    - Interactive Session: Discuss the impact of cultural dimensions on business practices.
    - Assignment: Students write a reflection on their country's entrepreneurial ecosystem.
- *Week* 2: Business Models and Strategic Planning
    - Workshop: Introduction to business models and strategic planning tools.
    - Group Activity: Students form multicultural teams to create a business model canvas for a startup idea.

  - Guest Speaker: An entrepreneur from one of the represented countries shares insights.

- *Week* 3: Innovation and Design Thinking
  - Seminar: Principles of innovation and design thinking.
  - Case Study Analysis: Groups analyze and present on a successful international startup.
  - Practical Exercise: Ideation session using design thinking methodology.

- *Week* 4: Marketing and Market Analysis
  - Lecture + Discussion: Global marketing strategies and consumer behavior analysis.
  - Project Work: Teams develop and pitch a market entry strategy for a product in a new country.
  - Video Conference: With a marketing expert from a multinational company.

- *Week* 5: Finance and Funding Strategies
  - Interactive Workshop: Understanding global financial resources and investment strategies.
  - Simulation: Financial planning exercise, including budgeting and forecasting.
  - Panel Discussion: Virtual session with international venture capitalists.

- *Week* 6: Leadership, Ethics, and Sustainability
  - Debate: On ethical dilemmas and sustainability challenges in entrepreneurship.
  - Leadership Workshop: Developing leadership skills for diverse and inclusive environments.
  - Final Project Presentation: Teams present their comprehensive business plans incorporating learned concepts.

Teaching Approaches:

- *Lectures for foundational knowledge.*
- *Interactive Sessions and Workshops for applying theoretical concepts.*
- *Group Activities and Projects to foster teamwork and practical application.*
- *Case Studies for critical thinking and real-world understanding.*

- *Guest Speakers and Panel Discussions to provide expert insights and global perspectives.*
- *Debates and Simulations for dynamic learning experiences.*

This curriculum is designed to be flexible, allowing for adjustments based on the specific interests and backgrounds of the students. By utilizing a wide range of teaching methods, the course aims to engage students actively, encourage the exchange of ideas, and prepare them for the challenges and opportunities of global entrepreneurship.

ChatGPT Screen

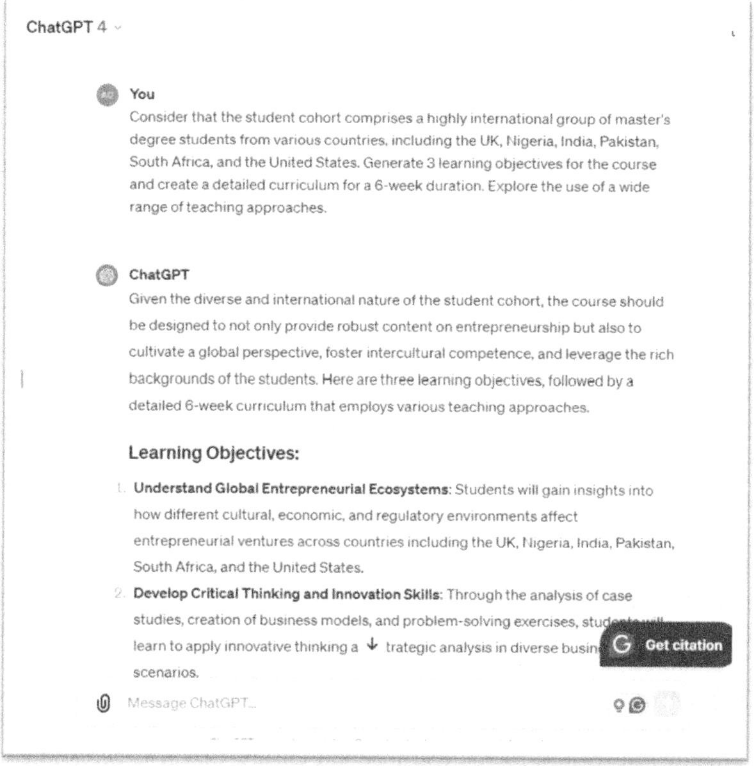

2.4 Case 2: Lesson Preparation

Beyond its utilisation in curriculum development, GenAI tools can be used in lesson preparation. Specifically, a tool like ChatGPT can be instrumental in two pivotal areas: the creation of a pre-teaching checklist and the formulation of lesson plans. Given the routinised nature of these tasks, ChatGPT offers substantial efficiency gains. However, the utilisation of GenAI as a tool in lesson preparation does not replace the educator's expertise and judgement but rather enhances it, by handling routine tasks and suggesting a broad range of options that can be fine-tuned to fit the specific context of the course. This synergistic approach ensures that educators can devote more time to the nuanced aspects of teaching that require human insight and creativity, ultimately enriching the learning experience for students.

Consider first the creation of a pre-teaching checklist. A pre-teaching checklist is a list of key items that an instructor should consider before preparing and delivering a teaching or learning session. It is a valuable tool for ensuring that the session is well-planned, effective, and meets the needs of the learners. In the creation of a pre-teaching checklist, GenAI can automate the aggregation of the essential components necessary for an effective teaching session. This includes logistical arrangements, such as ensuring the availability of teaching materials and technological tools, as well as pedagogical elements, like setting learning objectives and aligning them with the broader course goals. The ability of GenAI to swiftly process and organise vast amounts of information ensures that no critical step is overlooked, thereby streamlining the preparation process and enhancing the readiness of the educator.

The checklist may include items such as:

- Understanding the learning objectives: A teacher should have a clear understanding of the learning objectives and outcomes that they want to achieve in the session. This will help them to structure the session in a way that is effective and engaging for the learners.
- Knowing the learners: A teacher should consider the needs, backgrounds, and learning styles of the learners. This will help them to tailor the session to the learners and ensure that it is accessible and inclusive for everyone.
- Preparing materials and resources: A teacher should prepare all the necessary materials and resources for the session, such as handouts,

slides, and activities. This will help to ensure that the session runs smoothly and that the learners have everything they need to engage with the content.

- Planning activities and assessments: A teacher should plan activities and assessments that will help learners engage with the content and demonstrate their understanding. This will help to ensure that the session is interactive and that learners are actively involved in their own learning.
- Considering time and pacing: A teacher should consider the amount of time available for the session and plan the content and activities accordingly. This will help to ensure that the session is paced appropriately and that all the learning objectives are achieved within the time available.

Prompt 2.3 illustrates how ChatGPT produces the pre-teaching checklist for our postgraduate course on entrepreneurship. To generate this checklist, we provided information on the course, the curriculum, and the audience. This step would not be necessary if the checklist is being generated in the same session as the curriculum in Prompt 2.3. The prompt also illustrates how ChatGPT could be "put in the shoes" of the instructor: "*Consider that the student cohort comprises a highly international group of master's degree students from various countries, including the UK, Nigeria, India, Pakistan, South Africa, and the United States. What would you have on your pre-teaching checklist?*". The level of detail in the checklist provided by ChatGPT following the prompt is striking given the few seconds that it took ChatGPT to produce it. The list is not perfect, however. First, certain items may not be relevant in some contexts, and this is where human agency is required. Second, there is a subtle bias in the output. For example, without being informed, ChatGPT has assumed that the course will rely on a learning management system (LMS) and will take place online, although this may not be the case in resource-constrained contexts. Refining prompts, providing more contextual background, and running multiple iterations of a prompt will help to overcome this potential problem.

Prompt 2.3: How ChatGPT produces the pre-teaching checklist for our postgraduate course on entrepreneurship

Prompt

Consider that the student cohort comprises a highly international group of master's degree students from various countries, including the UK,

Nigeria, India, Pakistan, South Africa, and the United States. What would you have on your pre-teaching checklist?

ChatGPT Response
Creating a pre-teaching checklist for a diverse and international cohort of master's degree students involves several considerations to ensure that the course content is accessible, inclusive, and engaging for everyone. Here's a comprehensive pre-teaching checklist tailored for such a cohort:

1. Course Material Review and Localization
    - Ensure that the course materials (readings, case studies, examples) are relevant to and reflective of various international contexts.
    - Include content and examples from the represented countries (UK, Nigeria, India, Pakistan, South Africa, United States) to enhance relatability and engagement.
    - Verify that the course materials are accessible in terms of language and that technical terms are clearly defined.
2. Cultural Sensitivity and Inclusivity
    - Review the syllabus and course content for cultural sensitivity, ensuring that examples, discussions, and materials are respectful and inclusive of diverse backgrounds.
    - Plan for discussions and activities that leverage the diverse perspectives and experiences of the cohort to enrich learning.
3. Technology and Accessibility
    - Confirm that all students have access to the learning management system (LMS) and other digital tools required for the course.
    - Ensure that course materials are accessible to students with disabilities, including providing captions for videos and alternative text for images.
4. Communication Expectations
    - Establish clear communication guidelines, including preferred methods of contact, expected response times, and office hours that accommodate different time zones.

- Outline the expectations for student participation, especially in discussions and group work, considering the potential language barriers.

5. Group Work Dynamics

- Plan for forming diverse groups that mix students from different countries to foster cross-cultural collaboration and learning.
- Provide guidance on group work dynamics and conflict resolution, acknowledging cultural differences in communication styles and work ethics.

6. Pre-course Survey

- Conduct a pre-course survey to gather information about students' backgrounds, interests, and prior knowledge related to the course topics.
- Use the survey results to make any necessary adjustments to the course content and teaching strategies.

7. Pedagogical Strategies

- Prepare a variety of teaching strategies that cater to different learning preferences, such as lectures, case studies, interactive discussions, and practical projects.
- Plan for asynchronous learning activities and materials for students who may face challenges attending live sessions due to time zone differences.

8. Assessment and Feedback

- Design assessments that are fair and can accurately measure the learning outcomes across the diverse student body.
- Plan for a feedback mechanism that is constructive, timely, and culturally sensitive.

9. Orientation Session

- Schedule an orientation session to introduce students to the course structure, expectations, and available resources.
- Use the orientation as an opportunity to address any questions and to help students familiarize themselves with the digital learning environment.

10. Professional Development

- Engage in professional development activities related to teaching in multicultural and international classrooms to enhance your effectiveness as an instructor.

This checklist is designed to help you prepare a course that is not only educationally enriching but also culturally sensitive and inclusive, providing a supportive and engaging learning environment for your international cohort.

ChatGPT Screen

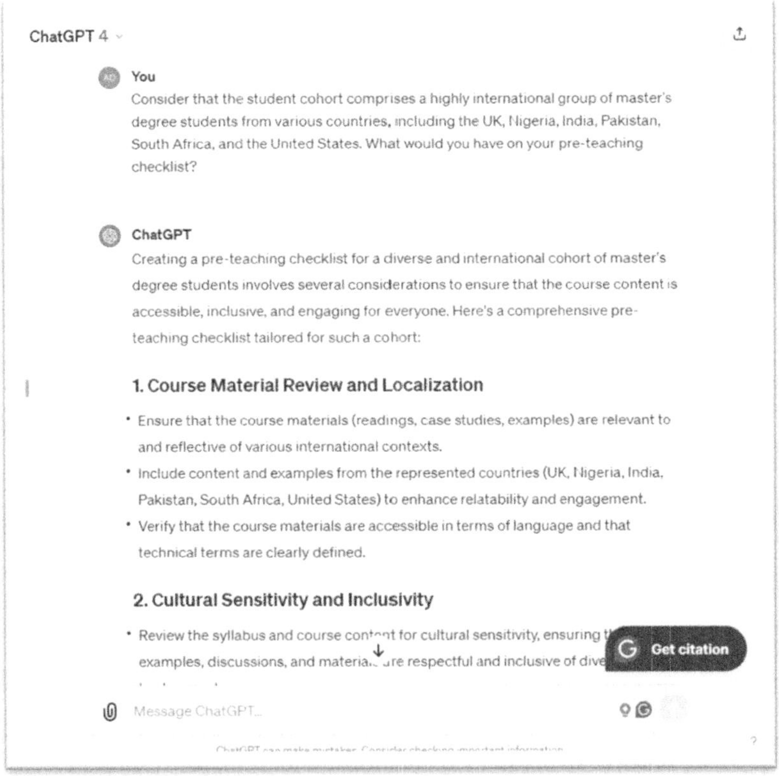

2.5 Case 3: Lesson Planning

Lesson plans are written documents that contain detailed information about a particular lesson or teaching session. In many ways, lesson notes and lesson plans are similar. They typically include the lesson objectives, materials needed, procedures, and assessment strategies. Lesson notes are important for teaching and learning for several reasons:

- Organisation: Lesson notes help teachers to organise their thoughts and ideas, and to structure the lesson in a logical and effective way.
- Preparation: Lesson notes help teachers to prepare for the lesson by providing a roadmap of what they need to do and what materials they need to gather.
- Consistency: Lesson notes help to ensure consistency in teaching. By having a detailed plan, teachers are less likely to forget important points or to deviate from the lesson plan.
- Timesaving: Lesson notes can save time in the long run by reducing the need for on-the-fly decision-making during the lesson.
- Assessment: Lesson notes provide a record of what was taught and how it was assessed, which can be useful in evaluating the effectiveness of the lesson and in making improvements for future lessons.

When making lesson plans, instructors can leverage the ability of GenAI tools to quickly create original content. Using their natural language-processing capabilities, these tools can recommend various activities and resources that fit the goals of a lesson and give teachers a strong starting point. They can also create detailed and clear lesson plans that teachers can adjust for students with different needs and backgrounds. To take advantage of the capabilities of the GenAI tools for lesson planning, the instructor may need to run several prompts. This could be because a lesson will be taught in several sessions and a separate plan is to be prepared for each session. It could also be to obtain additional details on different aspects of the lesson plan. For example, one may start with the broad instruction to create a lesson plan for a session on opportunity identification and business models, one of the topics suggested by ChatGPT in Prompt 2.4. The prompt reminds ChatGPT that this is a postgraduate course and we are planning for a 90-minutes lecture session.

For the context just described, Prompt 2.4 contains the full output of ChatGPT. By now the reader is expected to be familiar with the ChatGPT screen and it is therefore not reproduced henceforth. In generating the lesson plan, ChatGPT displays remarkable context-sensitivity. Without being told, it started out with a clear set of session learning objectives that link to the overall course learning objectives (see Prompt 2.4) and then based the session plan on them. This is what the expert instructor would do, and it should already be obvious that the output could be even more focused if the user provides some pre-defined learning objectives. The model's response should, of course, be used as a starting point for lesson planning. The instructor is expected to use the information provided to tailor their lesson plan to their learners' context, needs, and abilities. ChatGPT may as well be used to support this process. We may ask for, say, additional information and resources on specific topics or teaching methods. For instance, we may ask it to suggest a company with a unique or innovative business model which could be used as a case in the lesson.[2] By using tools like ChatGPT, the instructor will save a considerable amount of time in their preparation, but they still have the final responsibility to include activities, materials, and methods that will be most helpful to the learners.

Prompt 2.4: Lesson plan for a lecture session as generated by ChatGPT

ChatGPT Prompt

Create a lesson plan for "Business Models and Strategic Planning", the context is MSc program in Entrepreneurship and the approach is a 90 min workshop

ChatGPT Response

Creating a lesson plan for a 90-min workshop on "Business Models and Strategic Planning" for an MSc program in Entrepreneurship involves structuring the session to maximize student engagement and learning within a compact timeframe. Here's a detailed plan:

[2] When prompted with this, ChatGPT identified Airbnb which, in its words, "operates on a platform business model that connects hosts who have accommodations to rent with guests looking for a place to stay".

Lesson Plan: Business Models and Strategic Planning Workshop

Objective:

- Students will understand key components of successful business models and strategic planning processes.
- By the end of the workshop, students will be able to critically evaluate and develop business models and strategic plans for entrepreneurial ventures.

Materials Needed:

- Projector and screen for presentations
- Whiteboard and markers
- Handouts on business model canvas and strategic planning frameworks
- Case studies related to successful and failed business models (digital or printed)
- Laptops or tablets for student research (optional)

Workshop Breakdown:

- Introduction (10 min)
    - Welcome and brief introduction to the workshop's objectives.
    - Icebreaker activity: Quick roundtable where each student mentions a business model they admire and why (focus on diversity of industries and geographies).
- Part 1: Understanding Business Models (20 min)
    - Presentation (10 min): Overview of business models, introducing concepts like value proposition, customer segments, revenue streams, etc., using examples from well-known companies.
    - Activity (10 min): In small groups, students identify the key components of a given business model (using handouts or digital tools).
- Part 2: Exploring Strategic Planning (20 min)
    - Presentation (10 min): Introduction to strategic planning processes, emphasizing vision, goals, strategy formulation, implementation, and evaluation.

  - Discussion (10 min): Students reflect on a strategic planning case study, focusing on what contributed to its success or failure.
- Part 3: Integrating Business Models with Strategic Planning (30 min)
  - Group Activity (20 min): Each group selects an entrepreneurial idea (either pre-assigned or brainstormed in the session) and uses the business model canvas to outline its structure. Next, they draft a basic strategic plan outlining key strategies for achieving business objectives.
  - Group Presentations (10 min): Quick presentations by each group, sharing their business model canvas and strategic plan outline.
- Conclusion and Wrap-Up (10 min)
  - Recap of key learnings from the workshop.
  - Open floor for questions, encouraging students to think about how they can apply these concepts to their own entrepreneurial aspirations.
  - Provide information on further readings or resources for deepening their understanding of business models and strategic planning.

Assessment:

- Informal assessment through group activity participation and presentation.
- Provide constructive feedback on each group's business model canvas and strategic plan, highlighting strengths and areas for improvement.

Follow-Up:

- Recommend students to refine their business models and strategic plans as part of a course project, potentially leading to a pitch presentation.
- Offer office hours for students who wish to discuss their business ideas and plans in more detail.

This workshop is designed to be interactive and practical, ensuring that students not only learn theoretical aspects of business models and strategic planning but also apply these concepts through group activities and discussions.

ChatGPT Screen

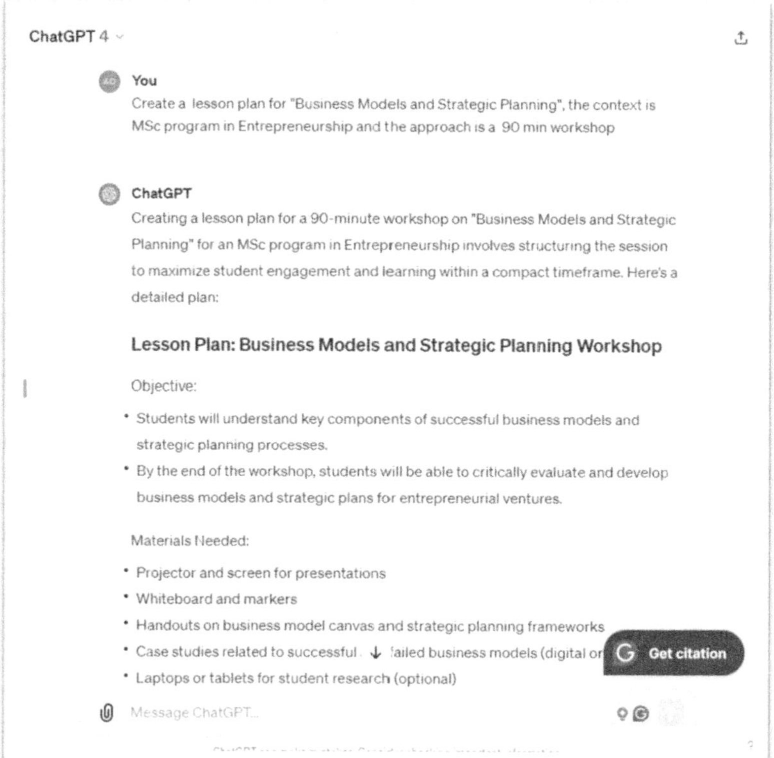

One important capability of ChatGPT that has been demonstrated thus far is its ability to remember previous prompts and responses and use this information to moderate current tasks. This feature makes interactions with ChatGPT more relatable and conversational.

2.6 Case 4: Course Content Generation: Slides and Interactive Activities

Chapter 1 already established the need for a dynamic teaching and learning pedagogy that capacitates graduates for lifelong learning in a rapidly changing labour market. One of the key challenges that educators face in this dynamic environment is how to create content that is not just relevant but also authentic and engaging for their students. Traditional content such as textbooks, lecture slides, and written assignments often fail to capture the attention and interest of learners who are accustomed to the interactive and personalised nature of digital media. Moreover, these methods may not adequately prepare students for the complex and dynamic problems that they will encounter in their personal and professional lives. To address this challenge, educators can leverage the power of GenAI tools like ChatGPT to create content that is adaptive, diverse, and immersive. By using these tools in conjunction with their pedagogical expertise and judgement, educators can design learning experiences that are relevant, authentic, and engaging for their students. And as GenAI becomes more advanced and accessible, the possibilities for educational content creation can only advance.

Presently, GenAI tools can already help educators create content that adapts to the needs, preferences, and goals of each student. Using natural language processing and machine learning, these tools can generate text, code, and other forms of content that match the level of difficulty, style, and format that suit each learner. For instance, ChatGPT can generate different versions of a text based on the reading level, background knowledge, and learning objectives of each student. This way, educators can provide personalised feedback and guidance to each learner, enhancing their motivation and performance. In addition, by drawing from a large corpus of data and sources, these tools can generate content that reflects a variety of perspectives, cultures, and experiences that may not be readily available or accessible to the instructor or the students. For example, ChatGPT can generate stories, poems, or essays that showcase the voices and views of different groups of people, such as women, minorities, or marginalised communities. This way, educators can expose their students to a range of ideas and opinions that can broaden their horizons and foster critical thinking. To sustain the interest of the learners, GenAI tools can help educators create content that is immersive and experiential—content that simulates real-world scenarios and situations that challenge the students to apply their knowledge and skills in authentic contexts. For instance, ChatGPT can generate dialogues, scenarios, or games that involve the students in role-playing, problem-solving, or decision-making activities that require them to use their creativity and logic. This way, educators can create content that not only teaches but also entertains and engages the students.

Moreover, a typical lecture or workshop session will feature different types of content, ranging from the more conventional multimedia slides to the more creative activities that require students to interact with themselves and with the instructor. As a starting point, the instructor will save a lot of time by prompting their GenAI tool to create either an outline or a full slide deck. A quick interaction with ChatGPT produces a 10-slide outline, a snippet of which is shown in Prompt 2.5. The prompt that produced this outline picks up on the learning objectives and lesson plan that we earlier generated. Specifically, ChatGPT was instructed as follows: "*Following the lesson plan for the workshop on 'Business Models and Strategic Planning,' create a PowerPoint slide outline and suggest a series of interactive activities at appropriate intervals to ensure sustained student engagement throughout the workshop*". However, it is entirely possible to start from scratch since our purpose is to create an outline that will not be copied wholly but will be adapted for the lecture.

Prompt 2.5: Generating ideas for workshop slides and activities

Prompt

Following the lesson plan for the workshop on 'Business Models and Strategic Planning,' create a PowerPoint slide outline and suggest a series of interactive activities at appropriate intervals to ensure sustained student engagement throughout the workshop.

ChatGPT Response

Based on the lesson plan for a 90-min workshop on "Business Models and Strategic Planning," here's a proposed PowerPoint slide outline along with a series of interactive activities designed to ensure active student participation and engagement throughout the session.

PowerPoint Slide Outline:

- Title Slide
    - Workshop Title: Business Models and Strategic Planning
    - Instructor's Name and Date
- Agenda
    - Overview of Today's Workshop
    - Objectives
    - Schedule
- Introduction to Business Models
    - Definition and Importance
    - Key Components of a Business Model
- Popular Business Models
    - Examples across Industries
- Introduction to Strategic Planning
    - Definition and Significance
    - Steps in the Strategic Planning Process
- Linking Business Models and Strategic Planning
    - How They Work Together
- Group Activity Instructions
    - Outline of the Activity
    - Objectives and Expected Outcomes
- Case Study Highlights
    - Key Takeaways from Successes and Failures
- Group Presentation Guidelines
    - What to Focus On
    - Time Allocation
- Conclusion
    - Recap of Key Learnings
    - Q&A
    - Further Resources

Interactive Activities:

- Icebreaker: Business Model Match-Up (10 min)
  - Activity: Distribute cards with different components of a business model (value proposition, customer segments, etc.) and have students match them to the correct definitions.
  - Objective: To familiarize students with the terminology and components of a business model in a fun, interactive way.
- Group Discussion: Strategic Planning Real-World Example (20 min)
  - Activity: After presenting a brief case study, facilitate a group discussion on its strategic planning aspects.
  - Objective: To encourage critical thinking about how strategic planning is applied in real-world scenarios.
- Hands-On Group Activity: Create Your Business Model Canvas (30 min)
  - Activity: Using the provided template, each group creates a business model canvas for a hypothetical or real startup idea.
  - Objective: To apply concepts learned in the workshop to a practical task, fostering collaboration and creativity.
- Quick-Fire Challenge: Strategic Planning Simulation (20 min)
  - Activity: Present a scenario (e.g., a sudden market change). Groups have 10 min to adjust their previously created business model canvas based on a strategic response to the scenario.
  - Objective: To simulate real-life strategic decision-making and adaptation under time pressure.
- Group Presentations and Feedback (10 min)
  - Activity: Each group presents their revised business model canvas and strategic plan adjustment. Provide constructive feedback.
  - Objective: To practice presenting business ideas succinctly and receiving feedback gracefully.

These interactive activities are timed to break up the workshop and keep engagement levels high. Each activity builds on the last, reinforcing learning objectives while encouraging participation, creativity, and critical thinking.

ChatGPT Screen

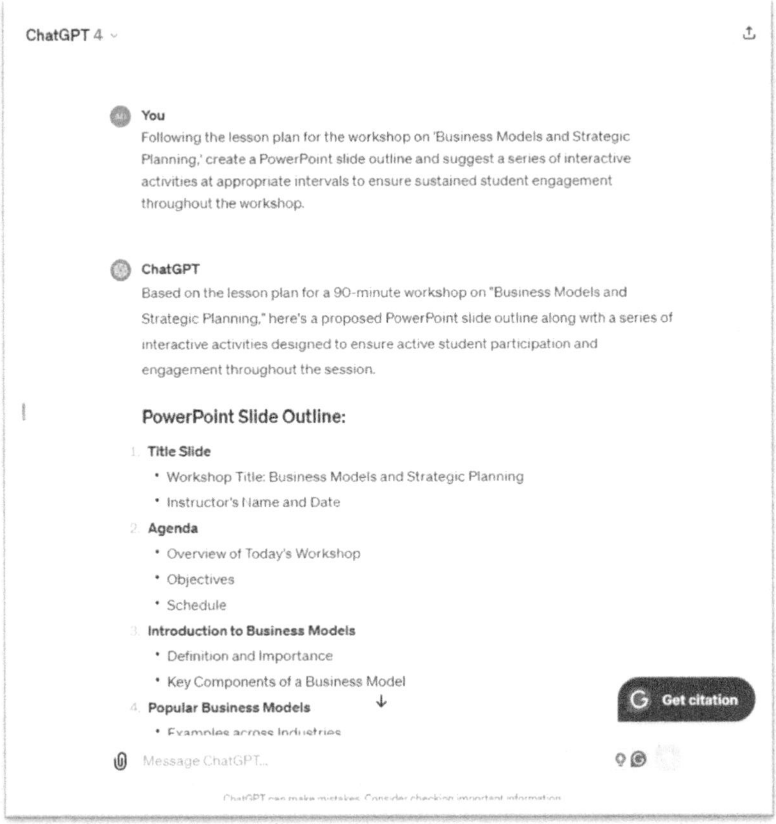

Beyond the use of slides or other static content as a medium of instruction, the most effective learning environments will incorporate interactive activities. These activities are a great way to engage students and promote active learning in the classroom. They can be designed to help students understand complex concepts, reinforce key ideas, and develop important skills. For example, an interactive class activity might involve students working in small groups to solve a problem, create a project, or participate in a simulation. By working together and using critical thinking skills, students can learn from each other, build on their knowledge, and develop a deeper understanding of the material. Additionally, interactive activities can be fun and entertaining, which can help to create a positive and engaging learning environment. This can be especially important for students who may struggle with traditional lecture-style teaching methods. For the content that we just created, we could readily integrate some interactive activities to create a more dynamic, effective, and enjoyable learning experience for students. To do this, we may focus on a specific kind of activity and ask ChatGPT to make suggestions.

Consider, for instance, the Business Model Canvas (Osterwalder, 2004; Osterwalder et al, 2005). We may want the students to learn the basics of this popular tool for business model development and analysis in a fun and interactive way. Normally, it would take a considerable amount of time and research to identify the right activities. GenAI tools do not remove the research responsibility from the instructor, but they reduce the time and effort that goes into it significantly. For example, we may start a session with ChatGPT with the prompt, "I want to help my MSc students to understand the Business Model Canvas. I want to do this with a fun and interactive class activity. What can you suggest?". Our run of this prompt generated a 3-hour activity titled "Innovate & Pitch: A Business Model Canvas Challenge". We would obtain something much shorter with the follow-up prompt, "This is an elaborate activity. I want something individual and fun but much shorter. Something they can quickly do in 5–10 min during a lecture". In response to this, ChatGPT returned "Rapid-Fire BMC Challenge Rapid Fire Business Model Canvas (BMC) Challenge", an activity "designed to be completed in 5–10 min, making it ideal for inclusion in a lecture. It encourages students to think quickly and creatively about business models in a fun and engaging way". The final solution is presented in Prompt 2.6, the output of the prompt, "I want you to generate a list of ideas between these two extremes. Up to 5 items will be fine. Use tabular format".

The instructor can impose their expertise and the reality of their teaching situation on these examples. Implementing these activities not only helps the delivery of content to students, it also creates an opportunity for students to learn ethical AI use. For example, the instructions within an activity like BMC Component Deep Dive might prompt students to utilise a designated GenAI tool or select one of their own. The presentations will offer an opportunity to reflect on their work and to critique the output of the GenAI tools. Consistent with what we describe in Kolade, Owoseni, and Egbetokun (2024), this approach takes student beyond the domain of know-what to know-how and show-how where students can demonstrate mastery of their subject.

Prompt 2.6: Generating list of 5-10mins interactive learning activities on Business Model Canvas (BMC)

Prompt
I want you to generate a list of ideas between these two extremes. Up to 5 items will be fine. Use tabular format.

ChatGPT Response
Certainly! Here are five engaging, individual activities that fall between the elaborate group workshop and a quick 5–10-min exercise. These activities are designed to enhance understanding of the Business Model Canvas in an interactive and fun way during a lecture:

Activity	*Description*	*Duration (min)*
1. Quickfire Challenge	Each student receives a card with one component of the Business Model Canvas (e.g., Value Propositions, Customer Segments). They have 2 min to jot down as many ideas as they can for a given business scenario	5–10
2. BMC bingo	Create a bingo sheet with BMC components and related terms. During the lecture, call out definitions or examples, and students mark their sheet. First to complete a line shouts "Bingo!" and briefly explains their choices	5–10
3. Flash case study	Present a very brief overview of a company's business model. Ask students to identify one component of the BMC based on the information (e.g., "What's the Customer Segment for Uber?"). They write their answer on a slip of paper	5–7
4. Component swap	Students write an idea for any BMC component on a piece of paper. Papers are then passed around every minute, and each student adds an idea for a different component that aligns with the initial suggestion, creating a mini-BMC by the end	5–10
5. Idea speed dating	Students think of a startup idea and choose one BMC component to focus on. They then share their idea with a partner for 1 min, switch partners, and repeat, focusing on how their component connects to different business ideas	5–10

These activities are designed to be engaging and insightful, offering students the opportunity to apply their knowledge of the Business Model Canvas in a variety of fun and interactive ways, within a short segment of your lecture.

ChatGPT Screen

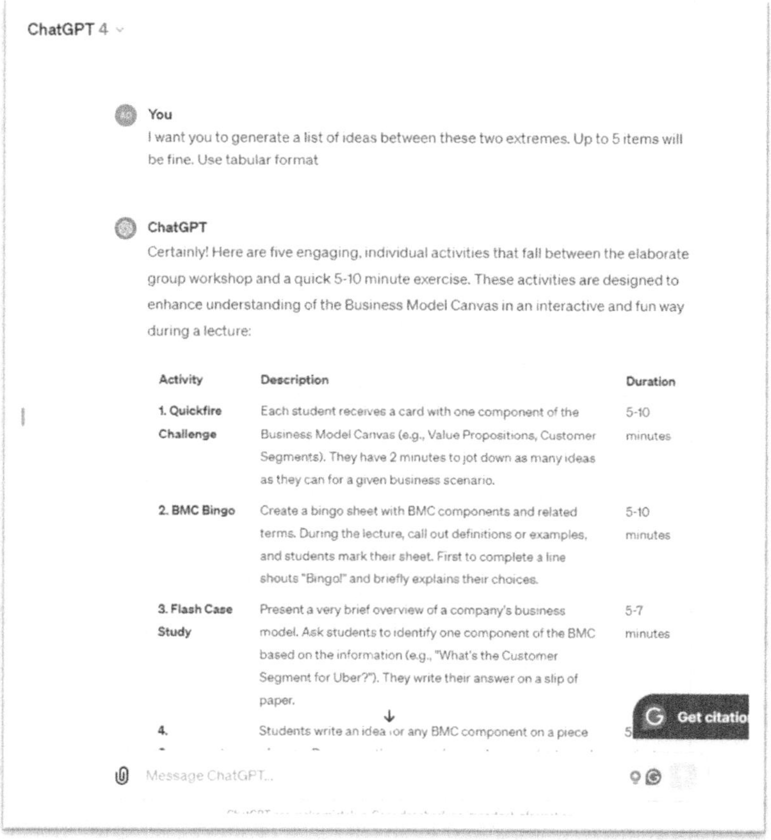

One thing that comes out from Prompt 2.5 is the relevance of group work and cases as elements of interactive teaching and learning. Case scenarios are frequently used in teaching and learning as a way to engage students and help them understand complex concepts and ideas in a real-world context. While working through a case scenario, students apply what they have learned in the classroom to a specific situation and see how the concepts and theories they have learned relate to real-world problems. This can make the material more relevant and meaningful to students and can also help them to develop critical thinking and problem-solving skills. Again, this is consistent with our proposition in Kolade, Owoseni, and Egbetokun (2024).

In a teaching and learning context, case scenarios can be used in a variety of ways, such as:

- Problem-based learning: Students work through a case scenario to identify and solve a real-world problem.
- Role-playing: Students assume different roles and work through a case scenario to understand different perspectives and make decisions.
- Simulation: Students work through a case scenario in a simulated environment to understand the dynamics of a situation and make decisions.
- Case study analysis: Students analyse a real-world case to understand the complexities of a situation and identify potential solutions to a problem.

Of all the uses of GenAI tools that have been covered so far in this chapter, drafting case material is the one in which the instructor will save the most significant amount of time. At the same time, it is the one in which the instructor's expertise is most needed, given the proclivity of large language models to sometimes misfire (Naddaf, 2023). Teachers could use, say, ChatGPT to generate ideas for case scenarios across a wide range of contexts, but they must prepare to check details thoroughly and learn to take the output for what it is—a starting draft to give ideas.

Let us return to our context of a postgraduate course in entrepreneurship, in which we are preparing a lesson on opportunity identification and business models. We asked ChatGPT to "create a case study that will be useful to illustrate the importance of opportunity identification in the process of entrepreneurship, highlighting the necessary skills that an adept entrepreneur should possess". The output shown in Prompt 2.7 is about a hypothetical startup created by two fictional entrepreneurs named Alex Johnson and Priya Singh. The opportunity that Alex and Priya spotted is the absence of affordable and efficient sustainable technology products for footwear. This is an interesting case not just because of its striking relevance to the topic but also because it picks up on another topical issue—sustainability. The draft explains that “Alex and Priya, both avid hikers and environmental activists, noticed a significant gap in the market. While the demand for sustainable products was growing, very few options existed in the footwear segment that genuinely adhered to eco-friendly principles”; they then proceeded to create a company that creates these solutions.

Prompt 2.7: Drafting a case scenario

Prompt
Create a case study that will be useful to illustrate the importance of opportunity identification in the process of entrepreneurship, highlighting the necessary skills that an adept entrepreneur should possess.

ChatGPT Response
Case Study: EcoStride Innovations—Pioneering Sustainable Footwear

Introduction
EcoStride Innovations emerged as a groundbreaking startup in the competitive footwear industry by capitalizing on an untapped market opportunity: eco-friendly and sustainable shoes. This case study explores the journey of its founders, Alex Johnson and Priya Singh, from identifying this unique opportunity to building a successful business that resonates with environmentally conscious consumers. It highlights the essential skills that made them adept entrepreneurs.

Opportunity Identification
In 2018, Alex and Priya, both avid hikers and environmental activists, noticed a significant gap in the market. While the demand for sustainable products was growing, very few options existed in the footwear segment that genuinely adhered to eco-friendly principles. They observed that consumers were becoming increasingly aware of environmental issues and were seeking products that aligned with their values.

- Key Skills Demonstrated:
  - Market Sensitivity: Understanding emerging trends and shifts in consumer behavior towards sustainability.
  - Innovative Thinking: Seeing beyond the current market offerings to envision a product that could meet an unaddressed need.

Market Research and Validation

To validate their idea, they conducted extensive market research, including surveys and focus groups. They discovered a strong desire for sustainable products, not just in their immediate community but globally. The feedback emphasized the importance of durability, style, and, crucially, the environmental impact of production processes.

- Key Skills Demonstrated:
  - Analytical Skills: Ability to conduct thorough market research and analyze data to inform their business model.
  - Communication: Engaging with potential customers to understand their needs and preferences.

Business Model Development

Using their insights, Alex and Priya developed a business model for EcoStride that focused on sustainability at every step – from sourcing biodegradable materials to implementing ethical manufacturing processes. They decided to use a direct-to-consumer model to maintain control over their supply chain and build a strong brand community.

- Key Skills Demonstrated:
  - Strategic Planning: Crafting a business model that aligns with their values and market demand.
  - Resourcefulness: Finding suppliers and manufacturers who shared their commitment to sustainability.

Overcoming Challenges

Launching EcoStride was not without challenges. The high cost of sustainable materials and the complexity of establishing a transparent supply chain were significant hurdles. However, Alex and Priya leveraged their problem-solving skills to innovate cost-effective solutions without compromising on their ethical standards.

- Key Skills Demonstrated:
    - Problem-Solving: Navigating the complexities of creating a sustainable supply chain.
    - Resilience: Overcoming setbacks and persisting in the face of obstacles.

Success and Impact
EcoStride Innovations quickly gained popularity, with its first line selling out within weeks of launch. Their success underscored the potential for businesses that not only offer innovative products but also contribute positively to the environment. EcoStride has since expanded its range, continuously innovating while maintaining its commitment to sustainability.

- Key Skills Demonstrated:
    - Adaptability: Evolving their product line based on consumer feedback and technological advancements.
    - Leadership: Inspiring a team and fostering a culture that reflects their mission and values.

Conclusion
The story of EcoStride Innovations serves as a powerful example of how identifying and pursuing the right opportunity can lead to entrepreneurship success. Alex and Priya's journey illustrates that a deep understanding of the market, combined with essential entrepreneurial skills such as innovative thinking, strategic planning, and resilience, can turn a vision into a thriving business that not only generates profit but also makes a positive impact on the world.

ChatGPT Screen

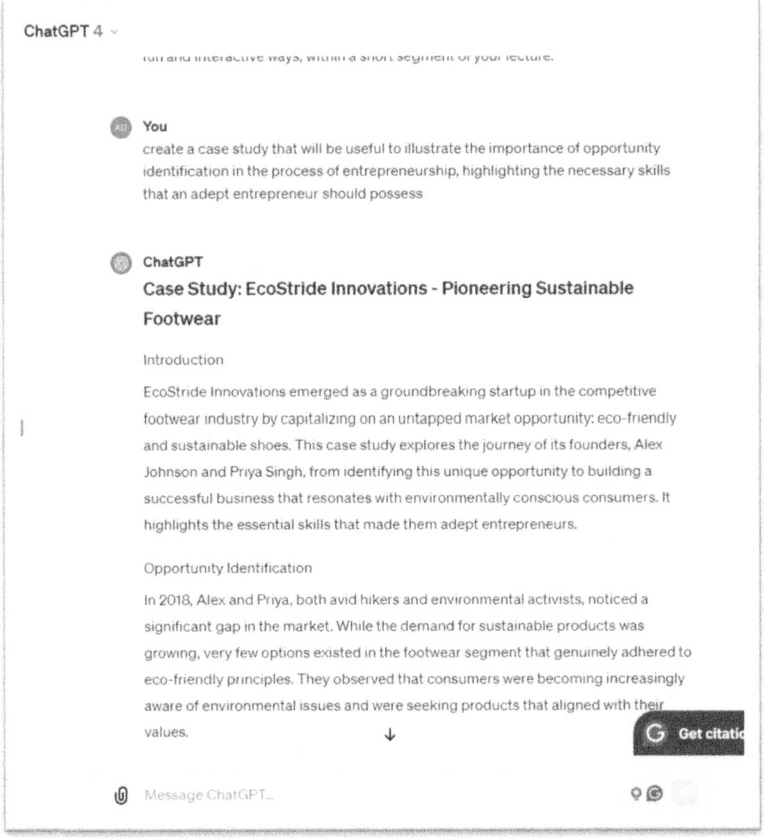

Instructors could hold a conversation with ChatGPT to expand on these initial ideas and even elicit suggestions on how the case could be delivered. Moreover, the cases that ChatGPT or any other GenAI tool will throw up may be too generic. The additional prompting will help to elicit further useful details. For instance, the hypothetical case could be swapped with a real one by supplying the name of an organisation to ChatGPT or asking it to specify an existing company. The latter is especially useful as it makes it easier for the instructor to cross-check data and triangulate information provided by ChatGPT. Similarly, further information could be elicited on specific aspects of the case. For instance, more information could be requested on the market competition that Alex's and Priya's startup had to face, its sources of initial investments and so on.

While the case study generated by ChatGPT may appear shallow theoretically, it appears to be a good starting point, which educators can build on or use in conjunction with other literature.

2.7 Conclusion

This chapter has illustrated the potential of Generative AI (GenAI) technologies to enhance the efficiency of lesson preparation and content development within the educational sector. GenAI tools like ChatGPT help to automate routine tasks and offer educators the opportunity to dedicate more time to specialised tasks that require their unique insights, creativity, and empathetic judgement. In addition to enhancing the efficiency of educational processes, this also enriches the learning experience for students. Ultimately, educators can invest the time that they save with GenAI tools in ensuring that education remains relevant, adaptive, and aligned with the demands of the twenty-first century.

Indeed, the synthesis of GenAI capabilities with human expertise presents a promising pathway toward impactful pedagogy. The inevitable result of the synthesis will be a deeply human-centric, effective, and innovative educational paradigm. Within this paradigm, technology and tradition will coalesce to prepare learners for the complexities of the modern world. Of course, there is a valid concern that technology threatens to replace the irreplaceable: human connection. However, GenAI is a partner, not a replacement. Imagine educators, empowered by GenAI, tailoring lessons to ignite each student's passion. A future where robots grade essays? Maybe. But robots cheering on a student's breakthrough moment? Not likely. Ultimately, the emphasis remains on the enduring value of the educator's role in guiding, interpreting, and contextualising the learning experience amidst rapid technological advancements.

References

Bloom, B., Englehart, M., Furst, E., Hill, W., & Krathwohl, D. (1956). *Taxonomy of educational objectives: The classification of educational goals. Handbook I: Cognitive domain*. Longmans, Green.

Kolade, O., Owoseni, A., & Egbetokun, A. (2024). Is AI changing learning and assessment as we know it? Evidence from a ChatGPT experiment and a conceptual framework. *Heliyon, 10*(4), 1.

Naddaf, M. (2023). ChatGPT generates fake data set to support scientific hypothesis. *Nature, 623*(7989), 895–896.

Osterwalder, A. (2004). *The business model ontology: a proposition in a design science approach*. Doctoral dissertation. Lausanne: University of Lausanne.

Osterwalder, A., Pigneur, Y., & Tucci, C. L. (2005). Clarifying business models: Origins, present, and future of the concept. *Communications of the Association for Information Systems, 16*(1), 1–25.

CHAPTER 3

Applications of Generative AI in Formative Learning and Assessment

3.1 Introduction

Formative assessment is a critical part of the learning process. Unlike summative assessment, which aims to evaluate students at the end of the instructional period, formative assessment provides ongoing feedback for learners throughout the instructional period. This enables learners to identify their strengths, reflect on their weaknesses, and make targeted efforts to improve. It also enables the tutor to adjust instructional strategies in response to student's needs, and to design, as and where appropriate, personalised learning plans. It is however inherently time and resource-intensive, and most higher education practitioners struggle to implement formative assessment plans, as they grapple with administrative and other responsibilities. Technology can therefore be much-needed help in this regard, helping educators to automate at least some of the formative assessment. Generative AI (GenAI) is especially primed for this, as algorithms can be trained with appropriate data to provide learners with massive feedback using, for example, interactive dialogues with the AI chatbot.

In this chapter, we will explore different techniques and approaches through which GenAI can be deployed to facilitate formative assessment and learning. These include the use of multiple-choice quizzes based on specific instructional materials to facilitate learners' grasp of key concepts;

A. Owoseni et al., *Generative AI in Higher Education*,
https://doi.org/10.1007/978-3-031-60179-8_3

training algorithms with materials that form the basis of interactive open-ended dialogues that help to develop students' critical thinking skills; and the use of GenAI to explore topics that are relatively more difficult to grasp. The chapter will also discuss the use of computer serious games for formative learning.

3.2 Context of Using Customised GPT for Formative Assessment

In the following sections, we will use a customised GPT created on ChatGPT to facilitate formative learning on the digitally enabled circular plastic economy in Africa. The GPT is trained mainly with a recent open access book on circular plastic economy, co-edited by one of this book's authors (Oyinlola & Kolade, 2023). It comprises sixteen chapters organised into three parts, so it can be likened to an average textbook used as a main reference material for a university undergraduate module. As well as the book, the GPT is also trained with two journal papers co-authored by one of the authors on the subject (Kolade et al., 2022; Oyinlola et al., 2022). The customised GPT, named Circular Plastic Economy GPT, can also draw from external web resources, but the training with peer-reviewed published content by the author is a firewall against inaccurate contents that the GPT could pick from the web. For good measure, the GPT was specifically instructed, among other things, to treat the uploaded book and journal articles as its primary sources, to which any additional external sources must align in terms of accuracy. It is important to note that instead of using online textbooks or journals, the instructor could upload self-generated lesson materials. However, we recommend that instructors should be mindful of potential copyright and ethical issues, such as the rights to use certain lecture materials.

The process of creating Circular Plastic Economy GPT is an exemplar that any interested educator can use to create customised GPTs of their own using, for example, a reference textbook as the main source material to train the GPT. It should be clarified that at the time of writing, creating a custom GPT is possible on only a handful of platforms like OpenAI's ChatGPT4 and Microsoft Copilot Pro, which often require a paid subscription. However, it is also important to clarify that, as an educator, you do not need to create a new GPT of your own to use generative AIs for formative learning. You can simply use or adapt existing GPTs. The additional appeal of custom GPTs comprise in the specificity of their training material and the better control that the creator has over content quality. The good news is that OpenAI has just announced, at the time of going to press in May 2024, that custom GPTs are now freely available to non-paid users, thus opening up new frontiers of creativity and impact.[1]

3.3 Case 1: How to Create a Custom GPT

Before proceeding with the rest of the sections in this chapter, we provide below a brief summary of the steps you can take to create a customised GPT on ChatGPT.

- **Step 1:** Sign up for a ChatGPT-4o account, the latest version (as of June 2024) freely available to all users. An advanced version of this 4o is available for paid users who can access more powerful features, including the ones for creating custom GPTs. However, you do not need to be a paid subscriber to access and use the custom GPT itself.
- **Step 2:** Click on "Explore GPT" menu on the top left-hand corner of your screen [see Fig. 3.1(1)]. In the centre of the screen, you will find a list of customised GPTs created by members of the public on various topics, organised by categories on the tabs. You can here use the search option to find a GPT on any topic of interest. The first tab is for "top picks" of the week.
- **Step 3:** On the top right-hand corner [Fig. 3.1(1)], click on "Create", next to "My GPTs". On the new page that appears, you will find two tabs in the left side of the page, the default for "Configure", and the other tab for "Create" (Fig. 3.2). You can use the "Create" tab to ask ChatGPT for suggestions based on what you want to do, otherwise you will mainly be using the "Configure" tab to customise your GPT. You can begin here by naming your GPT and provide a short description of what it does.
- **Step 4:** Provide detailed instructions for your GPT in the "instructions" section of the "Configure" tab. This is one of the most important sections in the creation of your GPT. Here, you need to provide detailed instructions on what the GPT should do, how

[1] Readers can access Circular Economy GPT via the following link: https://chatgpt.com/g/g-KxCjNWENW-circular-plasticeconomy-gpt.

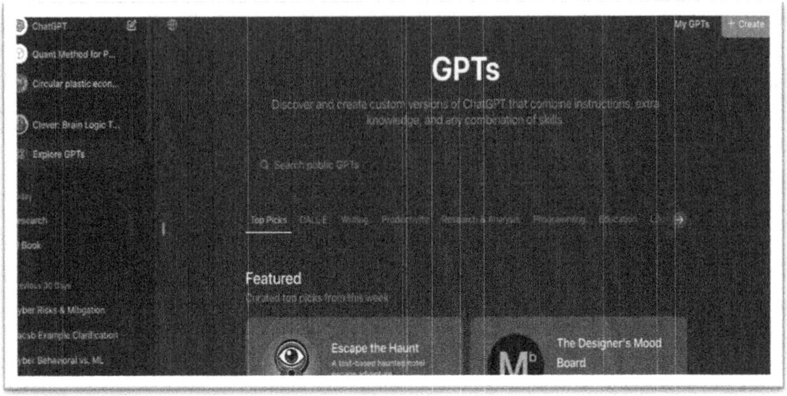

Fig. 3.1 Creating a customised GPT

it should do them, but also what it should not do. Figure 3.3 is an example of how this was done for the Circular Plastic Economy GPT. This is why the GPT creator can bring their creativity to bear to enrich the learner experience on the interface. Of course, you should test, run, and fine-tune your GPT in an iterative process!

- **Step 5:** In the knowledge section, upload resources you are using to train the GPT. As mentioned, for this chapter, we uploaded a 16-chapter open access book as our main, primary source, along with two journal articles [Fig. 3.3(3)]. Finally, include conversation starters which will appear as prompts for users on the frontend of your GPT, after you publish it.

3.4 Case 2: Interactive Quizzes for Formative Learning

The use of quizzes as a tool to engage learners is age long. Quizzes have a proven effectiveness to facilitate learners' understanding of key concepts, and they are often used for summative assessment. Their use for formative learning is relatively more recent and associated with technology interfaces like Socrative and Vevox, where they can be used in small group seminars. Generative AIs provide new opportunities to extend the creative use of interactive quizzes for formative learning.

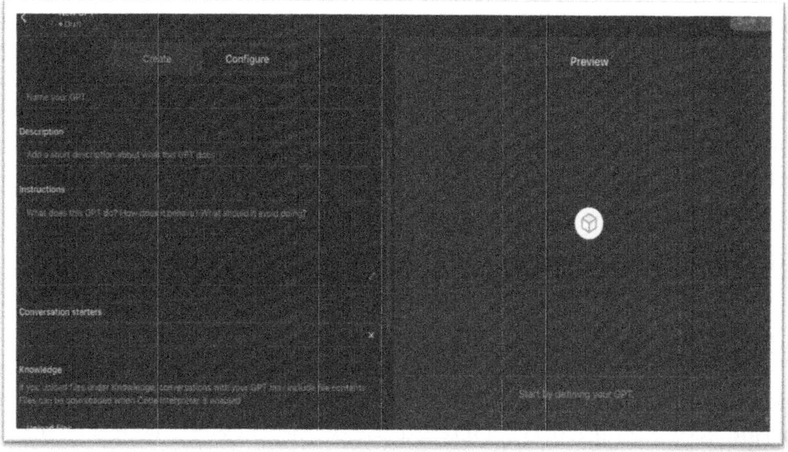

Fig. 3.2 Configure your GPT: name and description

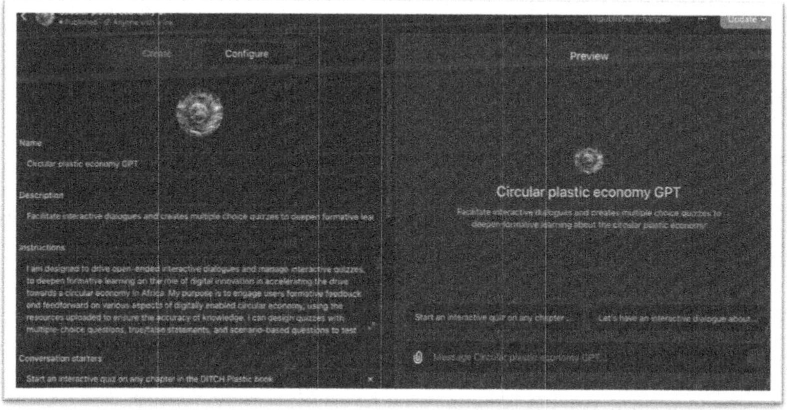

Fig. 3.3 Configure your GPT: instructions and knowledge sections

In the Circular Plastic Economy GPT, the GPT was provided explicit instructions to, for example, give the learner the opportunity to choose one of the sixteen chapters of the book they are interested in exploring, presumably after reading the chapter. It is then instructed to generate 20 questions, but take them one at a time, and to provide feedback for the learner on each question, whether or not they get the answer correctly. In addition, at the end of the 20-item quiz, the GPT is instructed to provide each learner with a proficiency score and to give them feedback and recommendations on areas they should focus more attention for further study.

Prompt 3.1: Start Conversation with Custom GPT

Circular Plastic Economy GPT Prompt
Start an interactive quiz on any chapter in the DITCH Plastic book.

Circular Plastic Economy GPT Response
The "DITCH Plastic Book" comprises 16 chapters, each focusing on various aspects of utilizing digital innovations to transition to a circular plastic economy in Africa. Here's a list of the chapters from which you can choose to start the interactive quiz:

1. Introduction: A Digitally Enabled Circular Plastic Economy for Africa
2. Enabling a Successful Transition to a Circular Plastic Economy in Africa
3. Digital Technologies and the Regime Complex for Plastics in Nigeria
4. From Polymers to Microplastics: Plastic Value Chains in Africa
5. Digital Innovation Ecosystem for the Circular Plastic Economy
6. Utilising Plastic Waste to Create 3D-Printed Products in Sub-Saharan Africa
7. Blockchains for Circular Plastic Value Chains
8. Transitioning to a Circular Plastic Economy in West Africa Through Digital Innovation: Challenges and the Way Forward
9. A Multi-Stakeholder Multi-Sectoral Approach to a Circular Plastic Economy in Eastern Africa
10. The Application of Digital Technology in Circular Plastic Economy in Southern Africa: Case Studies
11. BIG-STREAM: A Framework for Digitisation in Africa's Circular Plastic Economy
12. A Plastic Data Exchange Platform for Africa's Circular Plastic Economy Transition
13. Enhancing Decentralised Recycling Solutions With Digital Technologies

14. Assessing Plastic Circular Economy Policies and the Use of Digital Technology in Africa
15. Gender and Digital Innovation On Circular Plastic Economy in Africa
16. Conclusion: The Future of Digitisation for the Circular Plastic Economy in Africa

Please choose a chapter from the list above to begin the interactive quiz.

Circular Plastic Economy GPT Screen

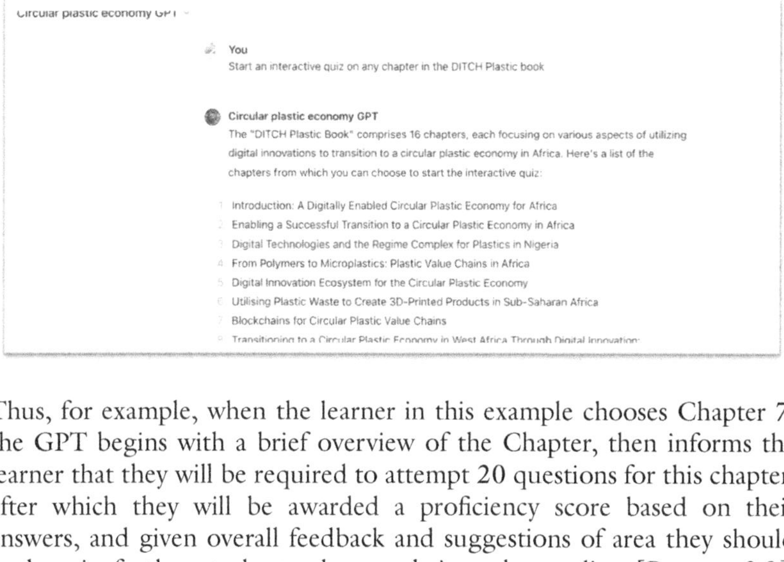

Thus, for example, when the learner in this example chooses Chapter 7, the GPT begins with a brief overview of the Chapter, then informs the learner that they will be required to attempt 20 questions for this chapter, after which they will be awarded a proficiency score based on their answers, and given overall feedback and suggestions of area they should explore in further study, to deepen their understanding [Prompt 3.2]. This is an example of application of generative AI to provide personalised formative learning. The organisation of the interactive quizzes on individual chapters enables the learner to focus on one topic at a time, similar to a lecture topic. And where, for example, a learner shows moderate level of proficiency, the GPT gives recommendations for further study based on those specific areas.

Prompt 3.2: Continued Interaction with Custom GPT—Select a chapter

Circular Plastic Economy GPT (Learner's) Prompt
I choose Chapter 7.

Circular Plastic Economy GPT Response
You've chosen Chapter 7: "Blockchains for Circular Plastic Value Chains" for your interactive quiz. This chapter delves into the transformative potential of blockchain technology in enhancing transparency, traceability, and trust within circular plastic value chains. It discusses the technology's fundamentals, its application across the plastic value chain's phases (design, production, use, and end-of-life), and a case study on BanQu's blockchain solution in partnership with Coca-Cola Africa for improving local recycling and driving a circular plastic economy in South Africa.

Let's start the quiz. Remember, you will attempt 20 questions, and at the end, you will receive a total proficiency score along with feedback and suggestions for further learning.

Question 1:
Which of the following best describes the role of blockchain technology in circular plastic value chains?

(A) To increase the use of fossil fuels in plastic production
(B) To reduce the transparency and traceability of plastic products
(C) To enable a centralized authority to control all data
(D) To enhance transparency, traceability, and trust across the value chain

Please choose the correct option (A, B, C, or D).

Circular Plastic Economy GPT Screen

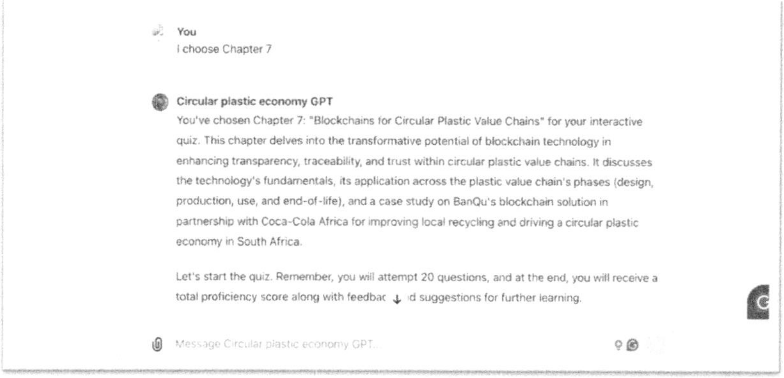

As the next iteration in the interactive quiz shows [Prompt 3.2], when the learner provides a response to the first question, the GPT first indicates whether the answer is right or wrong, then proceeds to give further explanations, irrespective of right or wrong answers. It then proceeds to the next question 2, prompting the learner, as before, to choose an option. In responding to question 2, we will choose a "wrong" answer to explore how the GPT will respond [Prompt 3.2]. What emerges here is already a departure from typical summative quizzes, where the learner is simply given their final score, and perhaps a list of right or wrong answers. By offering explications of correct answers, the GPT helps the learner to engage more deeply with the material. This is especially helpful when the learner chooses the wrong option, as exemplified in Prompt 3.2. Here, the algorithm also provides an opportunity for the learner to, for example, ask the GPT to explain more about why the initial answer chosen was deemed wrong.

Prompt 3.3: Continued Interaction with Custom GPT—Select a correct answer

Circular Plastic Economy GPT (Learner's) Prompt
Learner: D

Circular Plastic Economy GPT Response

That's correct!

Answer: D) To enhance transparency, traceability, and trust across the value chain.

Blockchain technology plays a crucial role in circular plastic value chains by enhancing transparency, traceability, and trust. It provides a decentralized and immutable ledger that allows for secure and verifiable tracking of plastic materials from production through to recycling and reuse. This capability is vital for establishing accountability and encouraging sustainable practices throughout the plastic economy.

Question 2:

What is one of the primary challenges blockchain technology addresses in the recycling and management of plastic waste?

(A) Decreasing the value of recycled plastics
(B) Increasing the complexity of plastic materials
(C) Facilitating the integration of informal waste collectors into the value chain
(D) Encouraging the production of single-use plastics

Please choose the correct option (A, B, C, or D).

Circular Plastic Economy GPT Screen

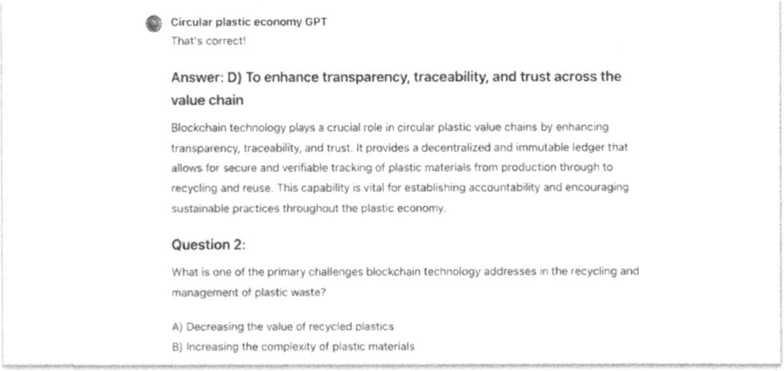

Prompt 3.4: Continued Interaction with Custom GPT—Select a incorrect answer

Circular Plastic Economy GPT (Learner's) Prompt
B

Circular Plastic Economy GPT Response
The answer provided is not correct.

Correct Answer: C) Facilitating the integration of informal waste collectors into the value chain.

One of the primary challenges that blockchain technology addresses in the recycling and management of plastic waste is facilitating the integration of informal waste collectors into the value chain. Blockchain can help formalize the contributions of these workers by creating a transparent and traceable record of their recycling efforts, thus enabling them to receive fair compensation and recognition for their work. This approach not only improves the livelihoods of informal waste collectors but also enhances the efficiency and effectiveness of recycling processes.

Question 3:
How does blockchain technology improve the transparency and traceability of recycled plastics?

(A) By allowing anonymous transactions without any records
(B) By creating a centralized database that only large corporations can access
(C) By documenting each step of the recycling process on a secure, immutable ledger
(D) By reducing the amount of information available about the origin and handling of plastics

Please choose the correct option (A, B, C, or D).

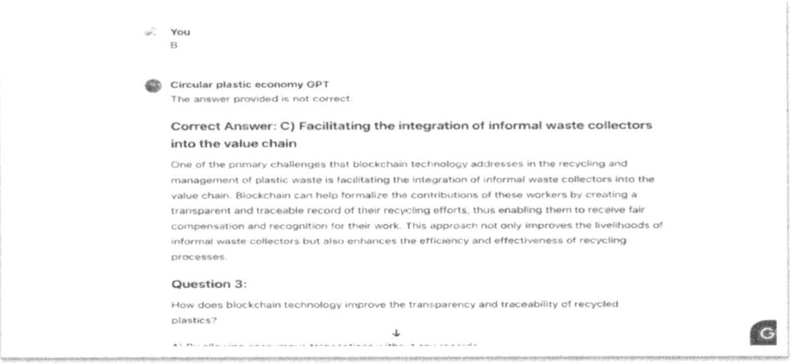

Circular Plastic Economy GPT Screen

The quiz progresses one question at a time until all 20 questions are attempted. At the end of this, the GPT awards "proficiency scores" for the chosen chapter using five levels: beginner (0–5 marks), intermediate (6–10), proficient (11–15), advanced (16–19), and expert (20 out of 20). As Box 3.5 shows, this proficiency score is followed by overall feedback and specific recommendations on areas the learner should study further to gain an even better understanding.

Prompt 3.5: Continued Interaction with Custom GPT—End of Quiz

Circular Plastic Economy GPT Prompt

(Not applicable)

Circular Plastic Economy GPT

You've completed all 20 questions of the quiz on Chapter 7: "Blockchains for Circular Plastic Value Chains". Let's calculate your score and provide feedback on your performance.

You've correctly answered **18** out of 20 questions. This gives you a score of 18 out of 20 marks.

Your level of proficiency is **Advanced**.

Suggestions for Further Learning:

- Revisit the concepts related to the challenges and barriers to blockchain adoption in the circular plastic economy, specifically focusing on overcoming the digital divide and the complexity of implementing blockchain solutions.

- Explore more about the potential synergies between blockchain and other digital technologies like IoT to further understand how they can collectively enhance circular economy practices.

Would you like to explore another chapter, or do you have any specific questions or topics in mind?

<u>Circular Plastic Economy GPT Screen</u>

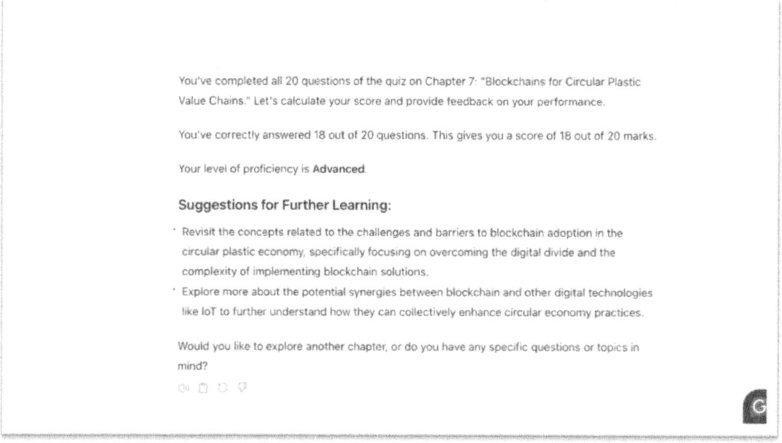

As we have seen, AI-enabled interactive quizzes offer myriads of benefits for learners, particularly in terms of their adaptability and real-time feedback for learners. The examples highlighted in this section are simple examples to illustrate some capabilities of generative AI for formative quizzes, but it is capable of much more. The algorithm can be trained to adapt questions to learners' levels of understanding, and then adjust the questions as the learners progress in their understanding of the instructional materials. It bears emphasising that generative AI offers tireless, unlimited feedback and feedback for individual learners, as and when required. This sort of time-intensive, personalised feedback is impossible for human tutors. So, deploying AI formative quizzes frees up time for human workers to spend on more creative tasks that generates better value for their time and skills. Furthermore, because the algorithm is trained with proven resources, customised GPT mitigates, if not entirely prevents, the risks of inaccurate content usually associated with general GPT products that draw all sorts of materials from the web. This enables learners' focused and efficient engagement with instructional materials.

In the next section, we will further explore the complementary benefits of formative dialogues. These are similar to formative quizzes in terms of opportunities for real-time feedback, but they are also distinct in that they are based on open-ended questions with no multiple-choice options.

3.5 Case 3: Generative AI-Enabled Formative Dialogues

In this case, we explore the innovative approach of using interactive dialogues to enhance learners' engagement with instructional materials. Emulating the Socratic Method, learners initiate the conversation by selecting a chapter from the instructional text and posing an open-ended question, which encourages active learning and critical thinking. The concise responses aim to keep the exchange lively and focused. This brevity also prompts learners to delve deeper, fostering a continuous, engaging dialogue. Importantly, each interaction concludes with a reflective query and a transition into related sub-topics, inviting further exploration. This technique not only ensures that learners are satisfied with the information provided but also subtly guides them through the chapter's breadth, drawing connections and enhancing comprehension. Through this method, the dialogue becomes a dynamic tool for discovery, using targeted follow-up questions to correct misunderstandings and build a robust understanding, all while maintaining alignment with the chapter's core content and supplementary web resources.

In Prompt 3.5, below, the learner uses the conversation starter to launch the dialogue. Here, similar to the interactive quizzes discussed earlier, the GPT is trained to respond by prompting the learner to choose any chapter in the book that they would like to explore further. For consistency of the demo and the opportunity to compare with the interactive quiz module, we choose Chapter 7, once again. Thus, when the learner responds in the next iteration with a simple "Chapter 7" in the dialogue, the GPT responds with an overview of that Chapter, after which it asks the learner about any other aspects of the chapter they want to explore. This gives the learner the control to explore specific concepts or areas they want to understand better, something that is likely to be different from learner to learner. This is an important advantage of customised AI algorithms: they provide multiple opportunities for personalised learning actively led by the learner. A human tutor cannot achieve this on the scale that the AI interface does.

The implementation of personalised learning programme is time- and resource-intensive, but it is nevertheless a critical instrument for achieving and raising outcomes for learners with varying types of experiences, interests, and other assets they bring to the learning space. Generative AI is therefore an effective and efficient system for implementing personalised learning. It is, in other words, excellently suited for asset pedagogies. By analysing learners' work to identify their unique skills and strengths, tutors can leverage on these insights to tailor their classroom teaching to build on these individual assets. Generative AI can also be used to develop a wide range of cultural perspectives and examples. In this particular example, the chapter being explored by the learner includes a case study from South Africa, made available because the GPT was specifically trained to include the example.

Prompt 3.8, Prompt 3.9, and Prompt 3.10 are exemplars of deep dive into aspects of the above dialogue.

Prompt 3.6: Deep Dialogue with Custom GPT (1)

Circular Plastic Economy GPT Prompt
Let's have an interactive dialogue about any chapter in the book.

Circular Plastic Economy GPT Prompt
Fantastic! Let's dive into a lively dialogue about one of the intriguing chapters from the "DITCh Plastic Book". Here are the chapters you can choose from:

1. Introduction: A Digitally Enabled Circular Plastic Economy for Africa
2. Enabling a Successful Transition to a Circular Plastic Economy in Africa
3. Digital Technologies and the Regime Complex for Plastics in Nigeria
4. From Polymers to Microplastics: Plastic Value Chains in Africa
5. Digital Innovation Ecosystem for the Circular Plastic Economy
6. Utilising Plastic Waste to Create 3D-Printed Products in Sub-Saharan Africa
7. Blockchains for Circular Plastic Value Chains

8. Transitioning to a Circular Plastic Economy in West Africa Through Digital Innovation: Challenges and the Way Forward
9. A Multi-stakeholder, Multi-sectoral Approach to a Circular Plastic Economy in Eastern Africa
10. The Application of Digital Technology in Circular Plastic Economy in Southern Africa: Case Studies of Waste Management Start-ups from Namibia and Zambia
11. BIG-STREAM: A Framework for Digitisation in Africa's Circular Plastic Economy
12. A Plastic Data Exchange Platform for Africa's Circular Plastic Economy Transition.
13. Which chapter sparks your curiosity, and what would you like to explore further within that topic?

<u>Circular Plastic Economy GPT Screen</u>

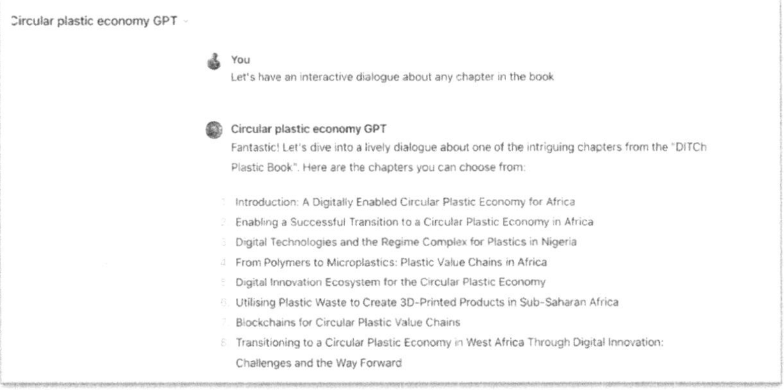

Prompt 3.7: Deep Dialogue with Custom GPT (2)

<u>Circular Plastic Economy GPT (Learner's) Prompt</u>

Chapter 7.

Circular Plastic Economy GPT Response

Great choice! Chapter 7, "Blockchains for Circular Plastic Value Chains," dives into an innovative area at the intersection of technology and environmental sustainability. Blockchains have the potential to revolutionize the way we track, manage, and verify transactions in the circular plastic economy, ensuring transparency, reducing fraud, and promoting responsible recycling practices.

Would you like to explore how blockchain technology can enhance transparency in plastic recycling processes, or are you more interested in understanding its role in incentivizing sustainable behaviors among consumers and businesses? Maybe you have another aspect of blockchain application in the circular plastic economy in mind?

Circular Plastic Economy GPT Screen

As the dialogue continues in Prompt 3.8 below, the learner asked to explore a specific context in the chapter: blockchain technology. Here again, we see a personalised example that is difficult to enact effectively in a classroom setting full of learners, where each person may want to dig deeper into different things, and a tutor cannot find enough equal time for all. In comparison with this customised GPT, a google search would bring up thousands of possible sources for the learner. The google search may be good as a complementary opportunity for further exploration, but cumbersome for more focused inquiry about a particular concept in a text.

Prompt 3.8: Deep Dialogue with Custom GPT (3)

Circular Plastic Economy GPT (Learner's) Prompt

I want to explore the idea of blockchain tokens. How can this be used to promote circular plastic economy?

Circular Plastic Economy GPT Response

Blockchain tokens hold significant potential to promote a circular plastic economy by creating a transparent, secure, and efficient incentive system for all stakeholders involved in the lifecycle of plastics—from manufacturers to consumers to recyclers. Here's how they can make a difference:

- Incentivizing Recycling and Responsible Consumption: Tokens can be awarded to individuals and organizations based on the amount of plastic waste they collect, recycle, or responsibly dispose of. These tokens can then be exchanged for goods, services, or even cash, motivating stakeholders to participate actively in the recycling ecosystem.
- Supply Chain Transparency: Tokens can be used to trace the journey of plastic products from their creation through to their end of life. This transparency can help verify that plastics are recycled and handled responsibly, encouraging trust among consumers and ensuring compliance with environmental standards.
- Encouraging the Use of Recycled Materials: Manufacturers who incorporate recycled plastics into their products can be awarded tokens, which could be used to demonstrate their commitment to sustainability. This system can encourage businesses to choose recycled materials over virgin plastics, thus supporting the demand for recycled content.
- Creating a Circular Economy Marketplace: The tokens can facilitate a marketplace where recycled plastics and products with recycled content are traded. This marketplace would not only provide financial incentives for recycling but also make it easier for businesses to source recycled materials, thereby promoting a circular economy.
- Reducing Plastic Pollution: By providing a tangible reward for recycling and responsible consumption, blockchain tokens can significantly reduce the amount of plastic waste that ends up in landfills and natural environments. This approach directly contributes to tackling the global issue of plastic pollution.

Would you like to dive deeper into any of these applications of blockchain tokens, or do you have any specific questions on how they can be implemented in practice?

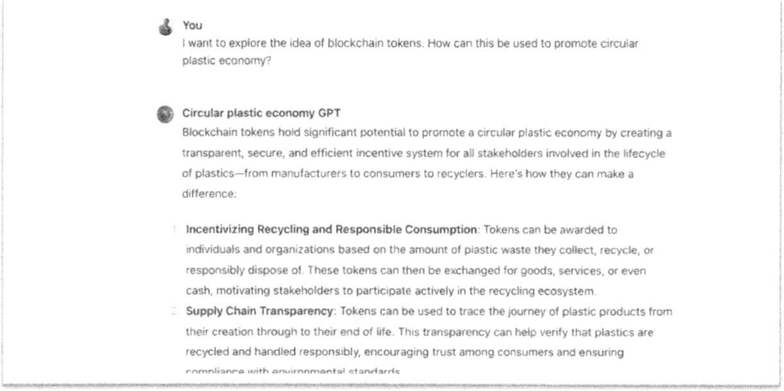

Languaging is another major issue, especially for international students learning in institutions away from their home countries, where other languages are used as means of instruction. This can become a barrier to learning and progression, including situations where learners have basic competence in a foreign language but are otherwise struggling with more technical concepts taught in foreign language. In the example in Prompt 3.9, the learner asks the GPT to explain a particular concept in Yoruba language, then Mandarin. This is the concept of Supply Chain Transparency mentioned in the previous response from the GenAI.

Prompt 3.9: Yoruba and Mandarin Language interpretation with Custom GPT

Circular Plastic Economy GPT (Learner's) Prompt

Please explain the concept of supply chain transparency in Yoruba Language and Mandarin.

Circular Plastic Economy GPT Response

English: In English, "Supply Chain Transparency" refers to the process of making every step from the procurement of raw materials, and manufacturing, to the final delivery of products to consumers, open and transparent to the external world within the entire supply chain. The purpose of supply chain transparency is to ensure that each operation can be tracked, monitored, and evaluated to improve product quality, protect workers' rights, reduce environmental impacts, and ensure that businesses and suppliers comply with relevant laws and ethical standards. By enhancing the transparency of the supply chain, consumers can make more informed purchasing decisions, while businesses can also enhance their brand image and market competitiveness by demonstrating their commitment to social responsibility.

Yoruba: Nínú èdè Yorùbá, ìm`ọ òye nípa "Supply Chain Transparency" túm`ọ sí "Síhànm`ọ Pínpín Àwọn Ohun Ìní" tàbí "Àfihàn Àwọn Ilànà Pínpín". Ó túm`ọ sí ìlànà tí a fi ń ṣe àfihàn gbogbo àwọn igbesẹ tí a gbà láti gbé ọjà tàbí iṣ´ẹ kan láti olùpèsè dé ọw´ọ alábàák´ẹgb´ẹ, p`ẹlú ìdí àti bí w´ọn ṣe gbà ṣe é. Èyí nípa kíkó àwọn alábàák´ẹgb´ẹ nínú pínpín ọjà tàbí iṣ´ẹ m`ọ nípa orísun àwọn ọjà, bí a ṣe ń ṣàkóso wọn, àti ìpèsè wọn. Ìdí pàtàkì fún "Síhànm`ọ Pínpín Àwọn Ohun Ìní" ni láti dáàbò bo àwọn `ẹt´ọ àwọn oṣiṣ´ẹ, ìdènà àwọn iṣ´ẹ àìm`ọ dáradára, àti láti ríi dájú pé àwọn ìlànà àyíká dára ní gbogbo `ẹka pínpín. Ó tún ṣe ìrànl´ọw´ọ fún àwọn oníbàárà láti m`ọ dájú pé àwọn ọjà tí w´ọn ń rà wá láti orísun tí ó bójúmu àti pé w´ọn ṣe wọn ní `ọnà tí ó t´ọ.

Mandarin: 在普通话中，"Supply Chain Transparency" 被翻译为"供应链透明度"。这个概念指的是在整个供应链中，从原材料的采购、生产加工、到产品最终到达消费者手中的每一个环节，都能够对外界公开、透明地展示信息和过程。供应链透明度的目的是为了确保每一步操作都可以被追踪、监控和评估，以提高产品质量、保护工人权益、减少环境影响，并确保企业和供应商遵守相关的法律和道德标准。通过提高供应链的透明度，消费者可以更加明智地做出购买决定，同时企业也能通过展示其对社会责任的承诺来增强品牌形象和市场竞争力。

Circular Plastic Economy GPT Screen

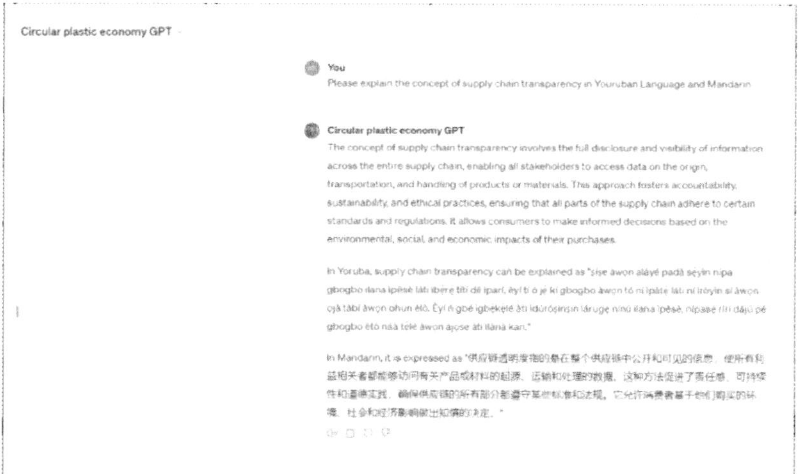

This language option enables students to dig deeper into concepts by exploring them in their mother tongue and circling back to the expressions used in the language of instruction. This is a prime example of GenAI-enabled asset pedagogy in action. The learner is able to harness the cultural asset of their mother tongue, along with the new asset of a foreign language of instruction, for a deeper understanding of a concept. The win–win process also enables them to strengthen their competence in both languages while immersing themselves in the subject being taught.

In the next iteration of the dialogue in Prompt 3.10 the learner wanted to explore a challenge that is not sufficiently covered in the book, that is, the disconnect between the high-end character of the technology and the imperative of access to low-income users. First, this is an example of a well-engaged, reflective learner with a desire to further explore the practical aspects of contents in the instructional material. The GPT was able to facilitate this level of immersive engagement, because it was trained not only with customised instructional material but also able to draw from external web sources as long as they align with the customised content. Here, the GPT was able to provide descriptions of low-tech solutions that do not require expensive smartphones or internet access. The learner could well go from here to explore additional sources on the web, but this formative dialogue gives enough information that would inform the direction of their search and further exploration. None of this can be achieved in a traditional classroom setting where multiple learners have different concepts and ideas they want to explore further.

To track and measure engagement with formative dialogues, the GenAI system can be trained to collect data on the dialogue interactions, including learner inputs, AI responses, and contextual information. The tutor can also analyse the structure and content of the dialogue interactions in order to improve the alignment between dialogue contents and the intended learning objectives.

Prompt 3.10: Explore challenge not covered in Custom GPT Knowledge base.

Circular Plastic Economy GPT (Learner's) Prompt

Blockchain tokens sound like a high-end technology that will be difficult for informal waste pickers to access. Many of them don't have smartphones, for example. So how can blockchains be used to empower lower-income informal waste pickers?

Circular Plastic Economy GPT (Learner's) Response

Indeed, the application of blockchain technology, particularly blockchain tokens, in empowering informal waste pickers poses challenges, especially considering the digital divide. However, there are innovative ways to bridge this gap and make the technology accessible and beneficial for lower-income informal waste pickers:

- Low-Tech Blockchain Interfaces: Develop simplified, low-tech interfaces for interacting with the blockchain. This could include using USSD codes (Unstructured Supplementary Service Data), which work on all types of mobile phones, not just smartphones. USSD codes can enable waste pickers to register collected materials, verify their transactions, and receive tokens without needing access to a smartphone or the internet.
- Community-Based Digital Access Points: Establish community access points equipped with the necessary technology where waste pickers can log their collections and transactions. These points can be located in community centers, recycling facilities, or cooperatives where waste pickers already bring their collected materials. Local NGOs or government bodies could support these hubs.
- Partnerships with Mobile Operators and Tech Companies: Collaborate with mobile operators and tech companies to provide affordable or even free access to the necessary technology. This could involve distributing low-cost smartphones, offering special data plans for waste pickers, or creating dedicated apps that are cost-free to access.
- Token Redemption Partnerships: Partner with local shops, cooperatives, and service providers to allow waste pickers to redeem tokens directly without needing a digital wallet. These partners can handle the digital aspects, allowing waste pickers to benefit from the token system through physical vouchers or ID cards.
- Education and Training Programs: Implement education and training programs to help waste pickers understand blockchain technology and its benefits. This education can focus on practical skills, such as how to use the technology to track collections and redeem tokens, and be conducted in partnership with local community organizations.
- Hybrid Models: Use a hybrid model that combines digital and physical tracking of collected materials. For example, waste can be logged digitally at collection points by representatives, with waste pickers

receiving physical tokens or receipts that can later be exchanged for digital tokens or directly for goods and services.

By addressing the technological and educational barriers, blockchain technology can be adapted to empower informal waste pickers, making them integral participants in the circular plastic economy. Would you like to explore any specific solution further, or do you have other concerns about the inclusivity of digital innovations in waste management?

Circular Plastic Economy GPT Screen

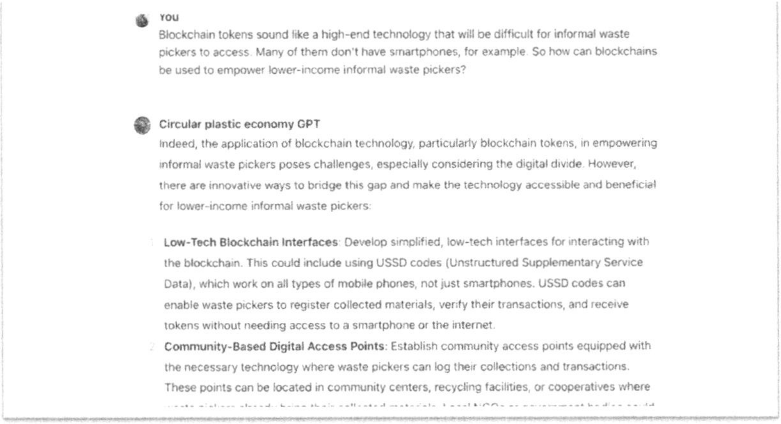

3.6 Case 4: Matching and Ordered Questions for Formative Assessment

Matching and ordered questions are versatile tools, particularly in the context of formative assessment, each serving distinct purposes yet equally valuable. These question types not only engage learners in active recall but also encourage the application of knowledge, making them apt for monitoring progress and understanding concepts during the learning process.

- **Matching Questions** offer a straightforward approach to assessing comprehension and the ability to associate related concepts with one another. This format typically involves a list of terms, phrases, or concepts on one side and a list of definitions, descriptions, or related items on the other, with the task being to match each item from the first list to its corresponding item in the second. The utility of matching questions lies in their efficiency in evaluating a learner's grasp of terminology, theories, and principles within a subject area. They are particularly useful in formative assessment because they can cover a broad range of topics quickly, providing immediate feedback on what learners know and what they struggle with. This immediate feedback is crucial for identifying areas that require further explanation or review, thereby facilitating a targeted approach to teaching and learning.
- **Ordered Questions**, on the other hand, test a learner's ability to sequence or prioritise information according to specific criteria. This could involve arranging steps in a process, ranking items by importance, or sequencing events in chronological order. Such questions demand a deeper understanding of the material, as learners must not only recall information but also apply logic and reasoning to organise that information correctly. In the context of formative assessment, ordered questions are particularly effective in assessing higher-order thinking skills and understanding of processes. They help instructors gauge not just what students know, but how well they can apply and analyse that knowledge in structured contexts. This insight is invaluable for adapting instruction to meet learners' needs and for guiding students in how to approach complex material systematically.

Both matching and ordered questions, by virtue of their design, promote active engagement with the material, requiring learners to make connections between concepts, apply logic, and demonstrate understanding in a structured manner. This makes them appropriate for formative assessment, where the goal is to inform both teaching and learning practices. Formative assessments aim to identify gaps in knowledge and comprehension early in the learning process, allowing for timely interventions that can enhance learning outcomes. By incorporating these question types, educators can provide varied and comprehensive assessments that not only measure knowledge but also stimulate learning, thereby enriching the educational experience and promoting academic success. Prompts 3.6

and 3.7 provide exemplars of how to use ChatGPT to generate ideas for matching and ordering questions.

Prompt 3.11: Create matching question

<u>**ChatGPT Prompt**</u>
Generate a matching question on the concept of digital transformation.

<u>**ChatGPT Response**</u>
Here's a matching question designed to assess understanding of various terms and concepts related to digital transformation. This format encourages learners to connect specific digital transformation elements with their definitions or implications:

Match the concepts on the left with their correct descriptions on the right.

Concepts:

- Digital Transformation
- Blockchain
- Big Data
- Artificial Intelligence (AI)
- Internet of Things (IoT)

Descriptions:

(A) A technology that enables the creation of decentralized and secure ledgers for transactions, reducing the need for intermediaries.
(B) The integration of digital technology into all areas of a business, fundamentally changing how it operates and delivers value to customers.
(C) The analysis and interpretation of large datasets to uncover patterns, trends, and associations, especially relating to human behavior and interactions.
(D) A field of computer science dedicated to creating machines capable of performing tasks that typically require human intelligence.
(E) A network of physical objects embedded with sensors, software, and other technologies for the purpose of connecting and exchanging data with other devices and systems over the Internet.

Answers:

B—Digital Transformation
A—Blockchain
C—Big Data
D—Artificial Intelligence (AI)
E—Internet of Things (IoT)

This matching question covers foundational concepts in digital transformation, testing knowledge on both the overarching process and specific technologies that facilitate or are part of this transformation.

ChatGPT Screen

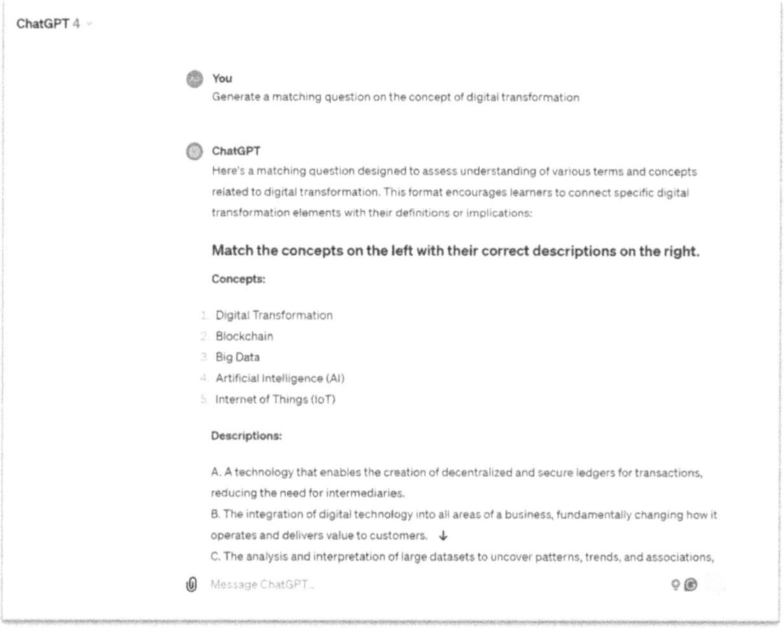

Prompt 3.12: Create ordered question

ChatGPT Prompt

Generate ordered question on the subject of digital transformation.

ChatGPT Response

Certainly, here's an ordered question that dives into the strategic approach towards digital transformation:

Question: Arrange the following steps in the correct order to effectively implement a digital transformation strategy within an organization:

(A) Deploying digital solutions across the organization.
(B) Evaluating the impact and refining the strategy.
(C) Identifying areas of the business that can benefit most from digital transformation.
(D) Developing a clear digital transformation strategy aligned with business goals.

Options:

1. C, D, A, B
2. D, C, B, A
3. A, B, C, D
4. D, A, C, B

Correct Answer: 1. C, D, A, B
This question encapsulates the strategic planning and execution phases of digital transformation, emphasizing the importance of initial assessment, strategic alignment, implementation, and continuous improvement.

ChatGPT Screen

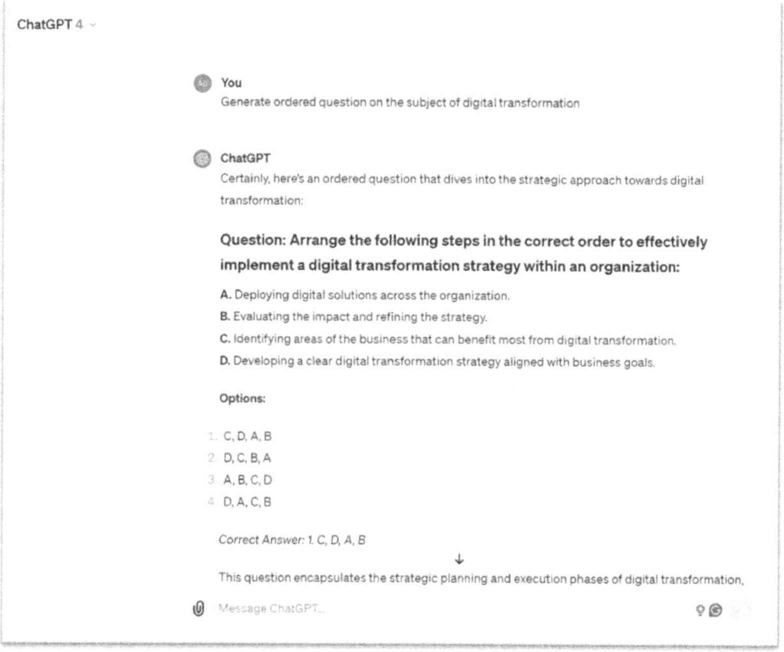

Note that Prompts 3.6 and 3.7 could be enhanced to provide a more comprehensive context. This could include specifying the number of questions contained within each prompt, detailing the level of difficulty of these questions, and incorporating additional demographic information about the learner's level of knowledge and diversity. Such enhancements would not only offer a clearer understanding of the intended audience and educational objectives but also enable a more tailored and effective learning experience. Providing these details can help in aligning the content with the needs and capabilities of the learners, ensuring that the educational material is both accessible and challenging enough to promote engagement and facilitate deeper understanding.

3.7 Case 5: Formative Serious Games

Computer serious games are games with purposeful learning at its core. They combine the fun and entertainment in casual games with specific educational objectives that often focus on skill development, skill acquisition, and critical thinking. Formative serious games focus on iterative skill development designed around specific real-life problems and scenarios, and the opportunities continuous feedback and feedforward in an iterative process. Simulation and serious games have been employed in the higher education sector for some time, although they tend to be limited to specific discipline, for example in Business and Management where tutors set up strategy simulation games for learners.

The recent incorporation of generative AI in serious games unlocks new opportunities for learners. Firstly, it offers a unique solution to the major gaps identified in higher education, in relation to industry, real-life experience opportunities for learners. AI-enabled serious games simulate scenarios and problems that imitate real situations that students are being prepared for. While this has significant usefulness and benefits for summative assessment, the focus of the present chapter is on formative learning. In this regard, AI-enabled formative serious games are typically designed to take the learner on an adaptive journey of discovery in which the algorithms attune and modify the game and level of difficulty in alignment with the progression of the learner. Simulated environments are inherently stimulating, leveraging interactive gameplay such as quests and rewards to capture learners' attention and keep their motivation at a high level. As the game evolves, so does the learner progress in their skill development and competence levels. In the simulated environment, learners can make decisions, solve problems, and experience the consequences of their actions. This immersive process deepens their understanding, enhances their competences, and helps them to retain key concepts and ideas in the context of application.

Formative serious games are also excellently suited for performance evaluation (show-how), beyond knowledge testing (know-what) and competence assessment (know-how). This, as mentioned in Chapter 1, is a higher level in the pyramid of assessment that is often difficult to implement in traditional classroom settings because they are generally expensive and resource-intensive. Consultancy projects are an example. These require the tutor to find companies that are willing to host the learner, but, more importantly, with the relevant kind of activities and sufficient levels of challenges aligned to learning outcomes. Even with these in place, most companies assigned to students in consultancy projects tend to focus on a streamlined set of activities aligned to their competitive strategies. Their focused and limited scope, while an advantage for the companies, can be a limitation for learners interested in experiencing a broader variety of problems and challenges. In an AI-enabled simulated environment, learners can test and showcase their evolving competencies in a variety of problem situations across multiple organisations and sectors—all in one go.

Below, we highlight four of the well-known platforms for AI-enabled serious games that provide various opportunities for formative learning. The list below is a wide spectrum of disciplines including Medicine, Business and Management, Sciences, and Information Systems.

- **Virteasy:** Virteasy[2] is an AI-enabled virtual reality platform specifically designed for dental education. It provides immersive simulations of dental procedures, mirroring real-life situations. Traditional clinical education offers practical training, of course. The distinctive advantages of AI-enabled serious games is that it is cheaper and resource-efficient for learners to work with virtual reality, and then complement this with practice with human patients. Learners can also engage with a broader variety of challenges in an AI-virtual reality game, and therefore use these interactive scenarios to hone their skills and track their own progress in a risk-free environment that prepares them for real-world clinical practice. The opportunities for formative feedback and feedforwards are endless in this immersive learning experience.
- **Simformer**: Simformer[3] is a gamified platform that provides business simulators for skill training in areas such as strategic management, core marketing, sales, finance, entrepreneurship, and supply chain, among others. Learners experience running their own virtual businesses. The AI-driven simulations enable real-time feedback, as students make strategic decisions, analyse market trends, and manage financial resources in the simulator. The hands-on business simulations help the learners to develop entrepreneurial skills, strategic

[2] For more details about Virteasy, you can visit: https://virteasy.com/.

[3] More details about Simformer can be found at; https://simformer.com/.

thinking abilities, and financial literacy. Simformer can be integrated with learning management applications to provide a unique e-learning experience and interactive tasks that can be tailored to each learner's needs and adjusted as the learner progress with the tasks.

- **Labster**: Labster offers virtual lab simulations across various scientific disciplines, including biology, chemistry, and physics. It allows students to learn by doing, but more importantly, moving at their own pace. Simulations and tasks are customised to students' needs and are adjusted to higher levels of difficulties as learners progress. Labster uses AI-powered simulations and gamified learning to motivate and challenge students to explore complex scientific concepts, conduct experiments, and analyse results in a virtual laboratory environment. It uses the best 3D visuals to immerse students in true-to-life tasks and support them to practise every step until they achieve mastery (Labster, 2024). With interactive feedback and guided learning pathways, Labster provides opportunities for formative learning and assessment, helping students develop critical thinking skills and practical scientific techniques.
- **CodeCombat**: CodeCombat is a platform that gamifies coding education, offering interactive programming challenges and puzzles for students of all skill levels. With AI-driven adaptive learning algorithms, CodeCombat uses AI-driven adaptive learning algorithms to provide personalised learning experiences, in line with individual learner needs and progress. Students can engage in hands-on coding exercises, debug programmes, and collaborate with peers in the virtual environment. By mastering coding concepts and algorithms in a gamified environment, students can develop computational thinking skills, problem-solving abilities, and coding proficiency, while receiving formative feedback to guide their learning journey.

3.8 Conclusion

This chapter discusses the various avenues and opportunities to deploy generative AI to facilitate formative learning. Firstly, we discuss the development of customised algorithms that are trained with specific course materials, thereby ensuring that interactive activities are tailored and focused in line with course objectives. This also helps to forestall the problem of inaccurate outputs and dialogues, to which GenAIs are often prone. At the same time, the customised GPTs can still draw from external web sources, but filtered with the customised course materials to ensure accuracy. Secondly, we discussed the specific use case in interactive formative quizzes. Unlike summative quizzes, whose purpose is to assess students' level of knowledge at the end of course, formative quizzes take a more dialogic approach, providing feedback on each question, even where the learner gets the right answers. It also provides general feedback at the end, including recommendations of specific areas for further studies.

Thirdly, we discussed a use case in formative dialogues, similar to formative quizzes in its interactive approach, but different in the sense that it gives the learner the control to choose which aspects of the course material they want to explore further, for example because they found it more challenging. The following dialogues are then tailored accordingly on the chosen topic. The chapter also touched on language, using the illustrative example of a learner requesting a GPT to explain a challenging topic in their mother tongue—in this case, Yoruba and Mandarin. Finally, we provided a list of some platforms that uses AI algorithms to enhance engagement and immersive learning for competence development and performance evaluation.

References

Kolade, O., Odumuyiwa, V., Abolfathi, S., Schröder, P., Wakunuma, K., Akanmu, I., Whitehead, T., Tijani, B., & Oyinlola, M. (2022). Technology acceptance and readiness of stakeholders for transitioning to a circular plastic economy in Africa. *Technological Forecasting and Social Change*. https://doi.org/10.1016/j.techfore.2022.121954

Labster. (2024). 3D Learning Simulations. Labster. Retrieved August 28, 2024, from https://www.labster.com/3d

Oyinlola, M., & Kolade, O. (2023). *Digital innovations for a circular plastic economy in Africa*. Routledge. https://doi.org/10.4324/9781003278443

Oyinlola, M., Schröder, P., Whitehead, T., Kolade, O., Wakunuma, K., Sharifi, S., Rawn, B., Odumuyiwa, V., Lendelvo, S., Brighty, G., Tijani, B., Jaiyeola, T., Lindunda, L., Mtonga, R., & Abolfathi, S. (2022). Digital innovations for transitioning to circular plastic value chains in Africa. *Africa Journal of Management, 8*(1), 83–108. https://doi.org/10.1080/23322373.2021.1999750

CHAPTER 4

Applications of Generative AI in Summative Assessment

4.1 Introduction

For a long time, summative assessments have been a cornerstone in the ever-evolving education landscape. By summative assessment, we refer to the evaluation of learners' academic performance at the conclusion of an instructional period, such as the end of a project, unit, course, semester, or academic year. It is often contrasted with formative assessment, which is ongoing and allows for continuous feedback and adjustment of teaching and learning strategies in line with learners' needs (Man Sze Lau, 2016). Summative assessments are typically structured and standardised, designed to measure each learner's achievement in relation to learning objectives and outcomes. Examples include final examinations, end-of-unit tests, dissertations, presentations, and portfolios.

While their exact forms have changed over time, summative assessments remain the standard way to evaluate learners' knowledge and determine whether learning outcomes have been achieved at the end of a unit or course. However, while summative assessments are an essential part of the educational process, they are most effective when used in conjunction with formative assessments, which provide ongoing feedback and support for learning (Man Sze Lau, 2016; Taras, 2009). In Kolade et al. (2024) we provide a discussion of how Generative AI (GenAI) tools influence assessments especially in higher education where

A. Owoseni et al., *Generative AI in Higher Education*,
https://doi.org/10.1007/978-3-031-60179-8_4

written essays are a widely used type of summative assessment. We highlight, for instance, the critique that summative assessments sometimes promote memorisation rather than understanding and application that are associated with deep learning (Rawlusyk, 2018; Dixson and Worrell, 2016).

However, the rapid diffusion of GenAI tools has significantly expanded the scope and potential of summative assessments to enhance learning. This is true despite the downsides associated with the use GenAI tools. Two downsides are worth noting here. Firstly, tools like ChatGPT and Google Gemini now make it easier for learners to cheat by passing off AI-generated work as their own. Secondly, dependence on GenAI tools could limit genuine learning, and this raises the question of where to draw the line. These concerns notwithstanding, the application of GenAI in summative assessment will enable innovation and effectiveness in education. By automating routine tasks such as question generation and grading, GenAI frees educators to focus on the specialised tasks that demand their unique skills and insights. This collaborative approach optimises educational outcomes and ensures that assessment remains both effective and deeply human-centred.

Contrary to the conventional critiques, recent research suggests that learners show positive attitudes and perceptions towards GenAI-mediated instruction and evaluation (Fathi et al, 2024). The capacity to create customised GPTs makes this even more interesting. As we show in the previous chapter (Chapter 3), instructors can create and train their own GPT based on specific content that is relevant to their learners. Such customised GPTs are a nimble way to teach and provide real-time feedback. And they are much faster at these than human instructors. Thus, the future of education appears not as a battleground between technology and tradition, but as a fertile ground for synergy. The goal of preparing learners for the challenges and opportunities of the future can be achieved more creatively and efficiently with, rather than despite, GenAI.

This chapter explores the application of GenAI in summative assessment, focusing on how to improve the quality and fairness of evaluations. We will consider some ways in which AI can enhance various aspects of assessment, from the creation of personalised tests to the provision of tailored feedback that help learners to improve.

4.2 The Context and Relevance of Generative AI to Summative Assessment

Before turning to a discussion of GenAI use cases in summative assessment, it is worthwhile to briefly discuss the importance of summative assessments and how AI could make them even better. Summative assessments are most widely applied to evaluate whether learners have achieved certain outcomes but there are several additional points of relevance. For instance, summative assessments offer way to keep learners accountable. Impending assessments at the end of a structured learning period is one of the reasons learners stay focused throughout the period. Moreover, summative assessments provide a formal certification of learners' achievements as a basis for progression to higher levels of learning or certification of final achievement.

In today's teaching and learning landscape, widely accessible GenAI tools could be applied in each area of importance as highlighted in Table 4.1. The content of the Box was generated with Microsoft Copilot. After creating the table, Copilot was quick to point out that "while AI has the potential to greatly enhance summative assessment, it's important to use it as a tool to support, rather than replace, human judgement and expertise". This is a stark reminder that, no matter how smart they become, AI tools are not likely to completely usurp the role of the human educator. This reminder is relevant today but even more so in the future for which today's education is preparing the learner. The World Economic Forum's Future of Jobs Report 2023 predicts that by 2027, 44% of workers' core skills will be disrupted due to the rapid pace of technological change, because technology is moving faster than companies can design and scale up their training programmes (Di Battista et al, 2023). The emphasis of education, and specifically of assessments, in this context should therefore transcend tests of what learners know—what we referred to as "know-what" in Kolade et al. (2024). Helping learners to acquire competence ("know-how") and demonstrate it ("show-how") should form the core of summative assessments. The rest of this chapter concentrates on illustrative cases of how educators can leverage GenAI tools to facilitate know-how and show-how.

Table 4.1 The importance of summative assessment

Importance of summative assessment	*How AI can facilitate*
Evaluation of learning outcomes	AI can provide a more nuanced and comprehensive evaluation of learning outcomes by analysing a wide range of learner data and generating detailed performance reports
Summative assessments provide a clear and objective measure of what a learner has understood and can do at the end of a learning period. They help in determining whether the learning objectives of the course or unit have been met	Example tools: Google Forms (for creating assessments), Google Classroom (for managing and tracking student progress)
Accountability	AI-powered platforms can track learner progress in real time, providing immediate feedback and holding learners accountable for their learning
Summative assessments hold learners accountable for their learning by providing a formal structure for evaluating their knowledge and skills. This can motivate learners to review and consolidate their learning	Example tools: Kahoot! (for creating fun, engaging learning games), Quizlet (for creating study sets and quizzes)
Feedback for educators	AI can analyse assessment data to provide educators with insights into the effectiveness of their teaching strategies, helping them make data-driven decisions
Summative assessments can provide valuable feedback for educators, helping them understand the effectiveness of their teaching strategies and make necessary adjustments for future instruction	Example tools: Edmodo (for tracking student progress and providing feedback), Socrative (for instant feedback on quizzes and checks for understanding)
Standardisation	AI can ensure the standardisation of assessments by eliminating human bias and error, leading to fairer and more consistent evaluations
Summative assessments provide a standardised measure of comparison between learners, classes, or schools, which can be useful for benchmarking and policymaking	Example tools: Turnitin (for plagiarism detection and ensuring academic integrity), Grammarly (for writing assistance and checking quality of written work)

(continued)

Table 4.1 (continued)

Importance of summative assessment	*How AI can facilitate*
Certification and progression	AI can automate the grading process, making it quicker and more efficient, which is particularly beneficial for large-scale assessments often used for certification and progression
Summative assessments often play a crucial role in certification and progression, as they provide a formal record of learners' achievement	Example tools: Grade scope (for consistent and efficient grading), Moodle (for creating and managing online courses)

Source: Extracted from conversation with Microsoft Copilot on 12 March 2024 (1500 GMT). Prompt: "I want to discuss assessment in higher education. Let's start with definition and importance of summative assessment"

4.3 Case 1: Exploring Summative Assessment Types

Chapter 3 already introduces the idea of custom GPTs that users can create and train in ChatGPT. Custom GPTs are useful in the domain of summative assessments. For example, a custom GPT can be trained on the content of a specific course or module, including handouts, written notes, texts, and reference materials used in teaching the course or module. The GPT can then readily be prompted to create summative assessment tasks that the instructor can modify and use. For example, a new GPT named *Africa Survey Sage* was created and trained for the purpose of a seminar on field surveys in Africa. The GPT was trained with two publications: an article on implementing surveys in Africa (Egbetokun, 2022) and an authoritative open-access text published by the World Bank (Iarossi, 2006). Both publications were required reading for the seminar and formed the basis for most of the teaching materials. The instructor can create a summative exam with the help of *Africa Survey Sage*. Prompt 4.1 illustrates how this might be done. The output, truncated due to space restriction, is a comprehensive set of questions that test learners' understanding at different levels.

Prompt 4.1: Creating Ideas for Summative Assessment (Examination)

ChatGPT Prompt

I want to create a summative exam on how to design and implement filed surveys in Africa. Propose a format that is appropriate for a cohort of international students studying in business management MSc in a UK business school.

ChatGPT Response

Exam Format: Summative Assessment

Part 1: Multiple Choice Questions (MCQs)—30%

- Objective: Assess basic theoretical knowledge and understanding of key concepts related to survey design and implementation in Africa.
- Structure: 20 MCQs, each worth 1.5 points.
- Sample Topics: Sampling techniques, challenges unique to the African context, ethical considerations, data collection methods.

Part 2: Short Answer Questions—20%

- Objective: Test students' ability to articulate insights on specific aspects of survey design and implementation.
- Structure: 4 questions, each worth 5 points.
- Sample Topics: Comparing and contrasting survey methodologies, discussing the implications of cultural diversity in survey design, strategies to enhance response rates in diverse African communities.

Part 3: Case Study Analysis—30%

- Objective: Evaluate students' ability to apply theoretical knowledge to real-world scenarios, focusing on problem-solving and strategic thinking.
- Structure: 1 comprehensive case study involving a scenario where students must design a survey for an African country, considering logistical, cultural, and ethical challenges. Students will be asked to outline their survey design, sampling strategy, and data collection plan.
- Assessment Criteria: Clarity of the survey objective, appropriateness of the methodology, consideration of ethical issues, and feasibility of the implementation plan.

Part 4: Essay Question—20%

- Objective: Measure students' critical thinking and ability to engage with complex issues related to conducting surveys in Africa.

- Structure: 1 essay question requiring a well-structured argument, supported by examples from literature or case studies covered in the course.
- Sample Topics: Discuss the impact of digital technology on survey methodologies in Africa, or evaluate the role of international organizations in supporting survey research in African countries.

Part 5: Reflection on Learning—Optional Extra Credit (up to 5%)

- Objective: Encourage students to reflect on their learning experience, highlighting insights gained and how they can apply this knowledge in their future careers.
- Structure: A short reflective essay on key takeaways from the course and how the student plans to incorporate this knowledge into their professional life.

ChatGPT Screen.

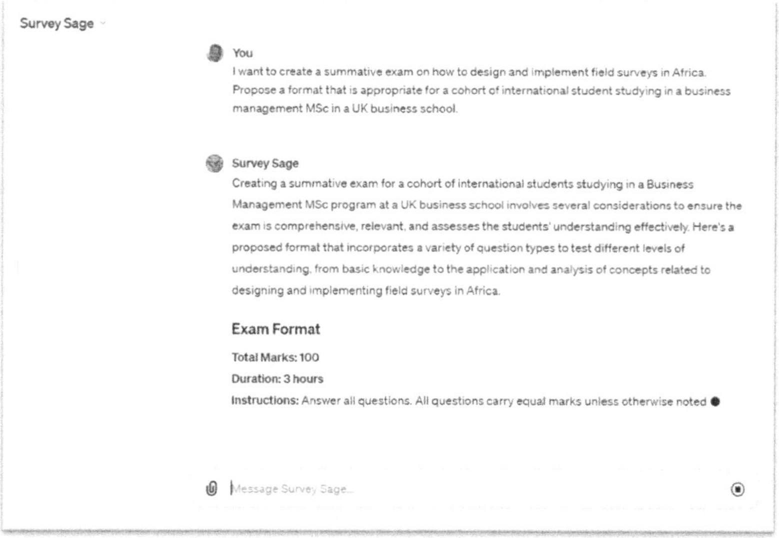

4.4 Case 2: Creating Multiple-Choice Summative Assessments

AI tools can support the instructor to speed up the rate at which tests, and assessment tasks are generated. For example, we could take our exercise from the preceding section forward by asking *Africa Survey Sage* to provide a variety of tasks within the summative assessment. The output generated from doing this is shown in Prompt 4.2. It includes a range of tasks in five parts that the instructor could modify to create a comprehensive assessment (Prompt 4.2). The collection of assessment tasks addresses theoretical knowledge, practical application, and critical thinking skills. The suggestions also include a clear objective and structure for each task as well as sample topics and assessment criteria for some of them. It is noteworthy that ChatGPT 4 provides a similar level of detail, but with less specific content compared to *Africa Survey Sage*.

Each of the assessment aspects in Prompt 4.2 can be expanded by following up with appropriate prompts. For example, we could ask it, or any other GenAI chatbot for that matter, to propose a set of multiple-choice questions (MCQs) for Part 1. For example, if we prompt Google Gemini with the specifications of Part 1 of our test, we get the output reproduced in Prompt 4.2.

Prompt 4.2: Ideas for a Multiple-Choice Test - Google Gemini

<u>**Google Gemini Prompt**</u>

I want to generate a summative test with the following specifications.

Type: Multiple Choice Questions (MCQs).

Objective: Assess basic theoretical knowledge and understanding of key concepts related to survey design and implementation in Africa.

Structure: 20 MCQs, each work 1.5points.

Sample Topics: Sampling techniques, challenges unique to the African context, ethical considerations, data collection methods.

Number of options per question: 4

Indicate the correct answer with an explanation.

Google Gemini Response

Sample Questions

1. Which sampling technique would be most appropriate for a researcher seeking to gather data from a widely dispersed rural population in an African country with limited infrastructure?

(A) Simple random sampling
(B) Cluster sampling
(C) Systematic sampling
(D) Quota sampling

Answer: B (Cluster sampling) Explanation: Cluster sampling allows for representative sampling when a complete list of the population is unavailable or logistically difficult to work from. It groups the population geographically for more efficient data collection.

2. A major challenge when conducting survey research in many African contexts is:

   (A) High levels of literacy
   (B) Reliable internet access across the population
   (C) Difficulty obtaining consent due to cultural norms
   (D) Uniformity of languages spoken

Answer: B (Reliable internet access across the population) Explanation: Limited internet infrastructure can create significant hurdles for online surveys and can impact data collection methods in general.

3. Which of these is a primary ethical consideration when implementing surveys in Africa?

   (A) Anonymizing collected data to protect participant identities
   (B) Ensuring the survey tool is offered in the dominant local language
   (C) Providing participants with a financial incentive for their time
   (D) Using open-ended questions to avoid limiting the participants' responses

Answer: A (Anonymizing collected data to protect participant identities) Explanation: While other options are important considerations, the protection of participant confidentiality is a foundational ethical principle of research.

4. A researcher aims to collect in-depth qualitative data about community perceptions of a new public health initiative in a sub-Saharan African country. Which data collection method is most suitable?

   (A) Online questionnaire
   (B) Telephone survey
   (C) Focus group discussions
   (D) Sampling of government records

Answer: C (Focus group discussions) Explanation: Focus groups facilitate the exploration of perspectives and experiences in a rich, nuanced way, well-suited to understanding community perceptions.

Google Gemini Screen

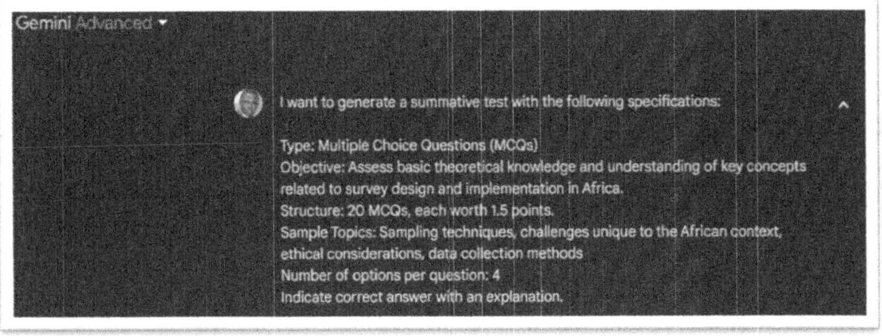

There are two important issues here. First, the human instructor needs to review both the proposed items and the options with a view to making changes as necessary. For example, the clarity of item 2 in Prompt 4.2 could be improved by modifying the options. The wording of option B, the correct answer, does not read like a challenge. Secondly, the tool obviously did not generate all 20 requested questions the first time. This issue is frequently encountered but it is not hard to circumvent. The user could readily expand upon the initial sample of items by asking for more. More generally, it may be more efficient to request for a large number of MCQs in small batches of, say, five items.

Interestingly, Google Gemini provided some unsolicited important considerations and additional tips which represent good advice. This reflects the expanding capabilities of GenAI tools to provide meaningful output. The important considerations include different aspects, namely:

(i) Distribution: How will you administer the test (paper-based, online platform, etc.)?
(ii) Question variety: Include questions assessing different levels of knowledge (recall, application, analysis).
(iii) Clarity: Ensure your questions and explanations are concise and unambiguous.
(iv) Alignment with learning outcomes: Make certain the test questions reflect the specific content covered in the survey design course.

For additional tips, Google Gemini recommended as follows:

(i) Start with a solid understanding of Bloom's Taxonomy to design questions of varying difficulty.
(ii) Get feedback from an expert familiar with survey design and African contexts to validate your test.
(iii) Pilot test your questions with a small group to ensure clarity.

4.5 Case 3: Creation of Personalised Summative Assessments

The above example, like typical assessments, does not take the diversity of learners into account. However, due to learner diversity, the creation of personalised summative tests should be seen as a crucial aspect of modern education. This is because today's learning environment is often internationalised and diverse. Especially in higher education, learners often come from diverse cultural backgrounds and possess varying abilities. In this context, we can think of several purposes that personalised tests serve. Firstly, they help to ensure that each learner's unique needs and circumstances are considered. Secondly, personalised tests can help to level the playing field such that all learners are assessed fairly and accurately. Thirdly, being tailored to match the learner's proficiency level, learning style, and cultural context, personalised assessment tasks provide a more accurate measure of the learner's understanding and skills. Finally, personalised tests can enhance learner engagement and motivation. When learners see that the assessments are tailored to their needs and reflect their learning journey, they are likely to become more invested in the learning process. This facilitates the transition from mechanistic learning to competence and application.

Artificial Intelligence (AI) can play a key role in the creation of personalised tests. For example, AI algorithms can analyse background data about a wide range of learners, including their past performance, learning preferences, and engagement levels. This data can then be used to generate assessments that are tailored to the learners' specific needs and abilities. For instance, if a learner struggles with a particular topic, the AI could generate additional questions on that topic to help the learner improve. If a learner excels in a certain area, the AI could provide more challenging questions to further stretch their abilities. The approach described here is not fundamentally different from the well-known computerised adaptive tests (CAT) used in standardised and certification tests, such as the Graduate Management Admission Test (GMAT), a globally recognised aptitude test. However, to calibrate them reliably, CATs require a considerable amount of "pilot" data, that is, a large pool of questions pre-tested on typical test takers (Wainer & Mislevy, 2000). For this reason, they are expensive to develop and are subject to major logistical, reliability and ethical concerns. The unparalleled ability of AI systems to analyse exceptionally large and complex data can help to overcome these problems. Admittedly, the implementation of such systems will require a sizeable initial investment, preferably at institutional level.

On a less sophisticated level, instructors can use commonly available GenAI tools to create personalised tests that take into account their students' cultural background, learning styles, and varied abilities. Such personalisation can take place on different scales. For example, the instructor may consider the different clusters within their student cohorts and develop summative assessments that reflect this differentiation. While this approach does not personalise the test at individual level (this is taken up in Chapter 5), it helps to make the assessment responsive to learners' group characteristics. To illustrate this approach, we will ask ChatGPT to generate an essay question on a topic, with variations based on students' language characteristics. Let us return to the subject of field surveys to illustrate how this may be done. An example prompt (Prompt 4.3) is as follows: *"I have a student cohort that comprises a group of 50 students. 30% of them are non-native English speakers. However, they are all required to take a final assessment comprising a 1000-word essay in English. The topic that has been taught is how to design and implement field surveys in resource-constrained contexts. Propose an essay topic for the student cohort, with two variations based on the students' characteristics".* This prompt (Prompt 4.3) generated an essay topic for each student group and the motivation for the topic. Instructors can leverage their expertise to structure the assessment and frame the topics appropriately.

Two observations can be made about the output of Prompt 4.3: One, the two topic variants are comparable in terms of how much effort the learners have to expend. Two, each topic takes advantage of the unique characteristics of the group of learners and challenges them accordingly. While the native speakers are challenged to think broadly about creative approaches to field surveys when resources are limited, the non-native speakers are challenged to think about the same problem but with a focus on language barriers with which they are likely to be more familiar. As illustrated in previous chapters, we may ask ChatGPT to produce the output in different languages or for learners with a learning disability, say, dyslexia.

Prompt 4.3: Ideas for Creating Personalised Exam

ChatGPT Prompt

I have a student cohort that comprises of a group of 50 students. 30% of them are non-native English speakers. However, they are all required to take a final assessment comprising a 1000-word essay in English. The topic that has been taught is how to design and implement field surveys in resource-constrained context. Propose an essay topic for the student cohort, with two variations based on the student characteristics.

ChatGPT Response

Given the diverse composition of your student cohort and the requirement to write an essay in English on the topic of designing and implementing field surveys in resource-constrained contexts, it's essential to consider essay topics that are accessible to all students while also allowing them to explore the subject matter deeply. Here are two variations of an essay topic designed to cater to the different characteristics of your students:

General Essay Topic:

"Challenges and Strategies in Conducting Field Surveys in Resource-Constrained Environments"

Variation 1: For Non-Native English Speakers

"Understanding and Overcoming Language Barriers in Field Surveys within Resource-Limited Settings"

This variation focuses on language barriers, which is particularly relevant for non-native English speakers. It encourages these students to explore and articulate their understanding of the complexities involved in conducting field research in environments where resources are scarce, and communication challenges might compound the difficulties faced. This topic allows them to draw from personal experiences or concerns related to language and communication, which can enrich their analysis and make the essay writing process more relatable and engaging.

Variation 2: For Native English Speakers

"Innovative Approaches to Data Collection and Analysis in Field Surveys Under Resource Constraints"

This version emphasizes the innovation and creativity required to effectively carry out field surveys in environments where resources are limited. It prompts students to think critically about methodological adaptability, technological solutions, and strategic planning to overcome such constraints. This topic is designed to push native English speakers to delve into more complex analytical and problem-solving aspects of the subject, encouraging a deeper engagement with the material.

By tailoring the essay topics to address specific aspects of the main theme, students can leverage their unique backgrounds and perspectives, ensuring that all students, regardless of their native language, can engage with the assignment in a meaningful way. This approach also fosters inclusivity and recognizes the diverse strengths and challenges of the student body.

ChatGPT Screen

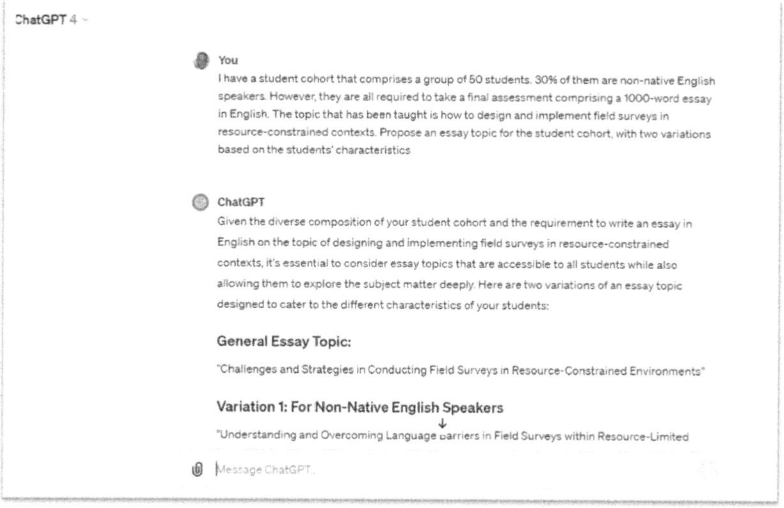

4.6 Case 4: Creation of Assessment Rubrics

An assessment rubric is a structured guide used to evaluate student performance against a set standard. Assessment rubrics provide a way to standardise the grading of assessments and make them transparent, fair, and consistent. Moreover, the use of rubrics helps to streamline the grading process, and to communicate clear and concise expectations for students. This clarity helps students understand what is expected of them and how they can achieve their learning goals. Thus, rubrics help to enhance the quality and impact of assessments. Also, rubrics help to provide feedback to both students and teachers, the former in terms of where their learning is deficient and the latter in terms of where teaching content and delivery could be improved. For these reasons, assessment rubrics have become a staple in the context of teaching and learning, especially in higher education (Chowdhury, 2019; Ragupathi & Lee, 2020; Reddy & Andrade, 2010).

Developing a reliable rubric is an involving process, especially the first time it is done for a particular course or module. From a practical point of view, there are several steps and considerations for the instructor (Table 4.2). A rubric must, first and foremost, match the learning outcomes that is being assessed. In Chapter 2 we discussed how ChatGPT could be used to support the development of learning outcomes. At the same time, the tool could be used to support the development of a rubric to assess students in relation to the learning outcomes. Notwithstanding, the expertise of the instructor is required in each step of the process. For example, to review and refine the rubric, the instructor may choose to pre-test it on a random set of students' work or ask for feedback from colleagues. These activities cannot be completely outsourced to AI.

In the remainder of this section, we will focus on illustrating how educators can save time by leveraging AI tools like ChatGPT in developing rubrics for summative assessment. However, beyond helping to develop rubrics, AI tools make it easy to implement ongoing updates and modifications to the rubric based on student performance and feedback. This ensures the assessment process stays relevant to students' changing needs and the overall learning goals in today's rapidly evolving educational context.

Table 4.2 Steps and considerations for developing an assessment rubric

Activity	*Description and purpose*
Identify learning objectives	Determine what skills or knowledge the assessment should measure. These should align with the overall learning objectives of the course or unit
Define performance criteria	Identify the specific criteria that will be used to evaluate student performance. These could include aspects like understanding of the material, application of knowledge, critical thinking skills, etc
Establish performance levels	Define different levels of performance for each criterion. These levels could range from "excellent" to "needs improvement" and should provide a clear distinction between different levels of student achievement
Assign points or grades	Allocate points or grades to each performance level. This provides a quantitative measure for each level of performance
Review and refine	Review the rubric to ensure it aligns with the learning objectives and provides a fair and comprehensive assessment of student performance. Make any necessary refinements before implementing the rubric

For our illustration, let us return to the personalised essay questions for native and non-native English speakers Prompt 4.3. A simple prompt could be passed to ChatGPT as follows: *"Generate a rubric for grading the essays. Use the grade range 0–39%, 40–49%, 50–59%, 60–69% 70–89% and > 90%"*. Note that this prompt does not include any information on learning objectives as this is expected to be embedded in the design of the assessment. Similarly, the prompt does not specify any performance criteria. However, in the output, part of which is pictured in Fig. 4.4, ChatGPT starts by defining six performance criteria upon which the rest of the output, the detailed rubric reproduced in Prompt 4.3 is based. It also attached a weight to each criterion.

This rubric contains the basic elements for comprehensive evaluation and feedback to students. From this point, the instructor has only two tasks: revising or adapting the performance criteria and editing the rubric as desired. For instance, the instructor may want to provide additional details under each grade range to offer more specific feedback to students regarding their strengths and weaknesses. It may be easier to do this in a table which we can generate by prompting ChatGPT to *"Bring the criteria and grade ranges together in tabular form. Put the grade range in columns and remember to indicate the weight of each criterion"*. The output of this prompt is reproduced in part in Prompt 4.3.

Prompt 4.4: Creating an assessment rubric

ChatGPT Prompt

Generate a rubric for grading the essays, use the grade range 0–39%, 40–49%, 50–59%, 60–69%, 70–89% and > 90%

ChatGPT Response

Grade Ranges

- > 90% (Outstanding)
    - Exceeds expectations in all criteria, demonstrating exceptional understanding, analysis, and application. Essays are

well-structured, with sophisticated language use and extensive evidence.

- 70–89% (Excellent)
  - Meets all criteria with high standards. Shows in-depth understanding and critical analysis, with strong application of theory. Essays are clearly structured and well-supported by evidence.
- 60–69% (Good)
  - Meets most criteria at a good standard. Demonstrates solid understanding and analysis with some minor gaps. Structure and use of evidence are adequate, with some room for improvement in language.
- 50–59% (Satisfactory)
  - Satisfactorily meets the basic requirements of the criteria. Shows understanding and some analysis but lacks depth. Structure and argumentation are adequate but could be enhanced.
- 40–49% (Marginal Fail)
  - Meets some but not all criteria, showing limited understanding and analysis. Structure is weak, and use of evidence is minimal. Language and style need significant improvement.
- 0–39% (Fail)
  - Does not meet the criteria. Lacks understanding of the context, with little to no analysis or application. Poor structure, minimal evidence, and numerous language errors.

ChatGPT Screen*

ChatGPT 4

You
Generate a rubric for grading the essays. Use the grade range 0-39%, 40-49%, 50-59%, 60-69% 70%-89% and >90%

ChatGPT
Creating a rubric for grading essays on designing and implementing field surveys in resource-constrained contexts involves establishing clear criteria that reflect the objectives of the assignment. The following rubric includes six criteria: Understanding of Context, Analysis and Critical Thinking, Application of Theory, Clarity and Structure, Use of Evidence, and Language and Style. Each criterion is graded on a scale reflecting the specified grade ranges, providing specific feedback aligned with the students' performance levels.

ChatGPT 4

ChatGPT
To present the grading rubric with grade ranges in columns and including the weight of each criterion, the table is structured as follows:

Criteria (Weight)	>90% (Outstanding)	70%-89% (Excellent)	60%-69% (Good)	50%-59% (Satisfactory)	40%-49% (Marginal Fail)
Understanding of Context (20%)	Exceptional understanding and insightful analysis of context-specific challenges.	Comprehensive understanding. Detailed analysis of context-specific challenges.	Good understanding. Some analysis of context-specific challenges.	Basic understanding. Surface-level analysis.	Limited understanding. Minimal analysis.
Analysis and Critical Thinking (20%)	Exceptional critical evaluation of methodologies with insightful connections.	Strong critical evaluation with clear connections.	Good level of critical thinking. Some evaluation of methodologies.	Basic critical thinking. Limited evaluation.	Limited critical thinking. Minimal evaluation of methodologies.
Application of Theory (20%)	Innovative and effective	Strong application of	Good application of	Basic application of	Limited or incorrect

Message ChatGPT...

*The second screenshot showed the output when ChatGPT was asked to present the rubric in a more tabular form.

4.7 Case 5: Grading and Feedback to Learners

Summative assessments are not an end in themselves. Rather, they form part of the overall teaching and learning experience the aim of which is to enhance the learner's knowledge, skills, and competencies. As part of the overall experience, learners will benefit from specific and actionable feedback that clearly highlights their strengths and weaknesses. In this sense, an educator can consider the learner's submission in response to summative assessment tasks as input into the pedagogy process. The concomitant output should be feedback on the submission. This is how learners will know what they are doing well and where they need to improve.

To provide feedback, students' work must first be scored. This is a non-trivial task especially where it involves written essays and large student cohorts. Apart from the widely discussed challenge that students sometimes submit AI-generated content, it takes a significant amount of time and effort to grade a large number of essays. It is even more demanding to provide personalised feedback that address each learner's needs. This is where automated essay scoring (AES) can be especially useful. As we argued in Kolade et al. (2024), it is "appealing to deploy AI tools in automatically scoring and providing feedback on assessment tasks such as essays and computer codes". This argument is consistent with previous research findings that automated assessments are indistinguishable from human grading and offer a potentially useful complement to the human teacher (Fathi et al, 2024; Vittorini et al, 2021). Even the more critical analyses (e.g., del Gobbo et al., 2023; Gardner et al, 2021) admit that AES systems are promising even if they are not yet sufficiently advanced for reliable assessment of higher-order learning as in written essays and oral presentations. This underscores the need for educators to complement rather than substitute key teaching activities with AI tools.

While current GenAI tools may not necessarily have all the capabilities of specialised AES systems, they have significant potentials that educators may already exploit. Thus, it is useful to reflect on the capabilities of existing AI tools to support grading and feedback to learners. For example, GenAI models like ChatGPT can be trained (see Chapter 3 on how to create custom GPTs) to understand the criteria of what makes an essay good or bad based on previous examples. This will not replace human judgement, but it will speed up the grading process by providing initial scores. It can also help in identifying strengths and areas that need improvement. Based on this, it can generate personalised feedback for each student. For example, if a student has not provided enough evidence to support their argument, the tool will point this out and suggest ways to incorporate more evidence. The remarkable ability of AI tools to consistently apply the same criteria is useful for ensuring the fairness of assessment and feedback. Instructors can take these as a basis for more detailed feedback based on their nuanced understanding, expertise, and critical thinking.

To illustrate, consider an essay topic that requires students to write on the relationship between human capital and economic growth. We start by asking ChatGPT to generate a rubric, using the exact same criteria, criteria weights, and grade ranges applied in the previous section. We then upload[1] an essay produced by one of the authors[2] and ask ChatGPT to grade it against the rubric and to generate detailed feedback (Fig. 4.6). The full grading and feedback are reproduced in Box 4.6. Clearly, the level of detail is extensive and beyond what the instructor wishes to manage, especially with large student cohorts. We could reduce the amount of detail generated by revising the prompt accordingly, limiting, for example to the overall grade and feedback.

It is also possible to use GenAI to support feedback to learners in a more interactive manner. For example, the instructor could provide a set of key evaluative statements and ask ChatGPT to generate a more elaborate write-up. Notwithstanding, as we have repeatedly emphasised throughout the book, the use of ChatGPT or any other GenAI tool cannot substitute for the expertise and nuanced knowledge of the human instructor. AI-generated feedback as typified in Prompt 4.4 should be taken as a starting point by the human instructor. The output itself creates the room for this, as the quantitative scores are provided in ranges and approximations rather than the single number that the human instructor needs to specify.

Prompt 4.5: Essay scoring with ChatGPT

ChatGPT Prompt

Apply the rubric to grade the attached essay. In addition to the overall score, provide detailed feedback on what is done well and what needs to be improved.

ChatGPT Response

Based on the detailed essay provided, here is the grading using the specified rubric:

[1] At the time of writing, the capability to accept uploaded files was not available in the free version, ChatGPT-3.5.

[2] See http://dx.doi.org/10.13140/RG.2.2.16248.87046. The essay was written more than a decade ago and is similar to a typical student essay.

- Understanding of Context (20%)
    - Grade: > 90%
    - Feedback: The essay demonstrates an exceptional understanding of the complex link between human capital and economic growth. The contextual review of growth models and empirical investigation specific to Nigeria shows comprehensive insights into the theoretical and practical aspects of human capital's role in economic development.
- Analysis and Critical Thinking (20%)
    - Grade: 70–89%
    - Feedback: The essay shows a very strong level of analysis and critical thinking, especially in how it critiques and compares various models of economic growth with human capital. However, some areas, such as the exploration of negative findings related to human capital accumulation, could benefit from deeper analysis to challenge or support existing theories.
- Application of Theory (20%)
    - Grade: 70–89%
    - Feedback: There is a very strong application of theoretical models to the empirical context of Nigeria. The essay skillfully navigates through complex theories, applying them to real-world data. Nonetheless, a more nuanced discussion on the applicability of these theories to diverse economic contexts could enhance the essay.
- Clarity and Structure (15%)
    - Grade: > 90%
    - Feedback: The essay is exceptionally well-structured, with a clear introduction, literature review, methodology, analysis, and conclusion. The logical flow and organization of content significantly enhance the reader's understanding and engagement with the topic.

  - Use of Evidence (15%)
- Grade: 70–89%
  - Feedback: The use of empirical data, especially from Nigerian sources, is very strong and well-integrated into the analysis. The essay effectively supports its arguments with evidence. Further diversification of sources and evidence, particularly from comparative international contexts, could provide additional depth.
  - Language and Style (10%)
- Grade: > 90%
  - Feedback: The essay is written in an engaging, clear, and precise academic style, virtually free of errors. The language used effectively communicates complex ideas and contributes positively to the essay's arguments.
  - Overall Score and Feedback
- Overall Score: 85%
- General Feedback: This essay stands out for its exceptional understanding and presentation of the link between human capital and economic growth, particularly within the Nigerian context. It excels in clarity, structure, and language use. To elevate the essay further, more critical engagement with the negative findings related to human capital accumulation and broader application of theory could provide additional depth and insight. Overall, this is an impressive analysis that contributes meaningfully to the academic discussion on economic development and human capital.

ChatGPT Screen

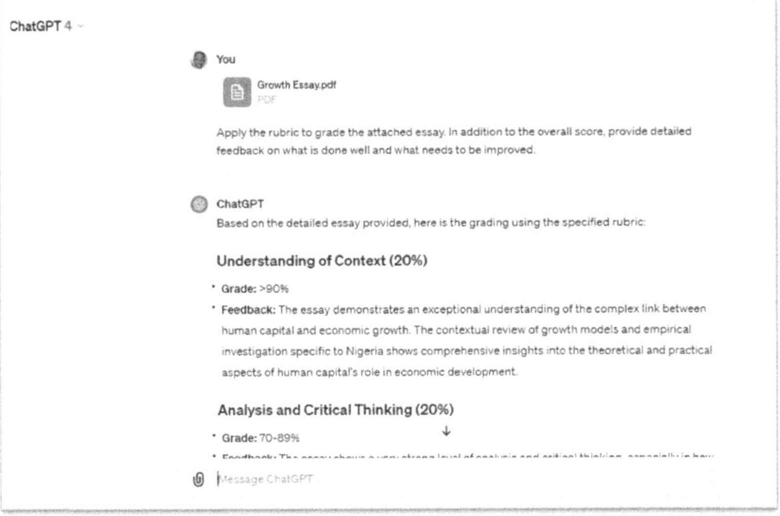

4.8 Conclusion

In this chapter, we have examined how the creation and grading of summative assessments could be enriched with GenAI. Indeed, the capacity of AI to automate routine evaluative tasks enables educators to dedicate more time to nuanced pedagogical engagements, thereby elevating the learning experience. Furthermore, custom GPTs enable personalised learning and assessment which help to optimise educational outcomes. However, our exploration of the application of GenAI in summative assessment does not ignore the challenges associated with these technologies, such as the risk of academic dishonesty and overreliance that could ultimately enfeeble the students. We acknowledge these challenges and emphasise the need for the human educator to take GenAI for what it is, an assistant rather than a substitute.

References

Chowdhury, F. (2019). Application of rubrics in the classroom: A vital tool for improvement in assessment, feedback and learning. *International Education Studies, 12*(1), 61–68.

del Gobbo, E., Guarino, A., Cafarelli, B., Grilli, L., & Limone, P. (2023). Automatic evaluation of open-ended questions for online learning. A systematic mapping. *Studies in Educational Evaluation, 77*, 101258. https://doi.org/10.1016/j.stueduc.2023.101258

Di Battista, A., Grayling, S., Hasselaar, E., Leopold, T., Li, R., Rayner, M., & Zahidi, S. (2023). *Future of jobs report 2023*. Geneva: World Economic Forum. https://www.weforum.org/reports/the-future-of-jobs-report-2023

Dixson, D. D., & Worrell, F. C. (2016). Formative and summative assessment in the classroom. *Theory Practice, 55*(2), 153–159. https://doi.org/10.1080/00405841.2016.1148989

Egbetokun, A. (2022). Conducting surveys in Africa: Reflections from national surveys in Nigeria. In O. Kolade, D. Rae, D. Obembe, & K. Woldesenbet Beta (Eds.), *The Palgrave handbook of African entrepreneurship* (pp. 573–594). Cham: Palgrave Macmillan. https://doi.org/10.1007/978-3-030-75894-3_23

Fathi, J., Rahimi, M., & Derakhshan, A. (2024). Improving EFL learners' speaking skills and willingness to communicate via artificial intelligence-mediated interactions. *System, 121*, 103254.

Gardner, J., O'Leary, M., & Yuan, L. (2021). Artificial intelligence in educational assessment: 'Breakthrough? Or buncombe and ballyhoo?' *Journal of Computer Assisted Learning, 37*(5), 1207–1216. https://doi.org/10.1111/jcal.12577

Iarossi, G. (2006). *The power of survey design: a user's guide for managing surveys, interpreting results, and influencing respondents*. Washington, DC: World Bank. http://hdl.handle.net/10986/6975

Kolade, O., Owoseni, A., & Egbetokun, A. (2024). Is AI changing learning and assessment as we know it? Evidence from a ChatGPT experiment and a conceptual framework. *Heliyon, 10*(4). https://doi.org/10.1016/j.heliyon.2024.e25953

Man-Sze-Lau, A. (2016). 'Formative good, summative bad?'—A review of the dichotomy in assessment literature. *Journal of Further and Higher Education, 40*(4), 509–525. https://doi.org/10.1080/0309877X.2014.984600

Ragupathi, K., & Lee, A. (2020). Beyond fairness and consistency in grading: The role of rubrics in higher education. In S. S. Shanger & N. W. Gleason (Eds.), *Diversity and inclusion in global higher education: Lessons from across Asia* (pp. 73–95). London: Palgrave Macmillan. https://doi.org/10.1007/978-981-15-1628-3

Rawlusyk, P. E. (2018). Assessment in higher education and student learning. *Journal of Instructional Pedagogies*, 21, 1. http://www.aabri.com/copyright.html

Reddy, Y. M., & Andrade, H. (2010). A review of rubric use in higher education. *Assessment and Evaluation in Higher Education, 35*(4), 435–448. https://doi.org/10.1080/02602930902862859

Taras, M. (2009). Summative assessment: The missing link for formative assessment. *Journal of Further and Higher Education, 33*(1), 57–69. https://doi.org/10.1080/03098770802638671

Vittorini, P., Menini, S., & Tonelli, S. (2021). An AI-based system for formative and summative assessment in data science courses. *International Journal of Artificial Intelligence in Education, 31*(2), 159–185. https://doi.org/10.1007/s40593-020-00230-2

Wainer, H., & Mislevy, R. J. (2000). Item response theory, item calibration, and proficiency estimation. In H. Wainer, N. J. Dorans, R. Flaugher, B. F. Green, & R. J. Mislevy (Eds.), *Computerized adaptive testing: A primer* (pp. 61–100). Milton Park: Routledge.

CHAPTER 5

Enhancing Personalised Learning and Student Engagement Using Generative AI

5.1 Introduction

Learning is inherently a personal journey, despite traditional educational models often presenting it as a collective experience within shared spaces like classrooms. This perception is even more pronounced when considering that assessments and evaluations are conducted on group and/or individual basis; however, no institution awards a group diploma, subtly underscoring the intrinsic value of recognising and addressing the personalised needs of each learner. Personalised learning emerges as a response to this, advocating for educational approaches that are tailored to the individual needs, interests, skills, and aspirations of each student. By moving away from the one-size-fits-all model, personalised learning embraces the diverse backgrounds, learning styles, and paces at which students absorb and engage with new information. It seeks to make learning more relevant and engaging by closely aligning educational experiences with each student's unique learning goals and preferences.

Mainstream pedagogical frameworks, such as Universal Design for Learning (UDL), reflect the importance of accommodating the individual variability in how students engage with content, process information, and demonstrate their understanding. The UDL framework (Kose, 2021) is built upon three foundational principles designed to offer multiple means of:

A. Owoseni et al., *Generative AI in Higher Education*,
https://doi.org/10.1007/978-3-031-60179-8_5

- **Engagement**: Encouraging learners' interest and motivation by providing options for self-regulation, effort, and interest enhancement.
- **Representation**: Offering content in varied formats (e.g., text, audio, visual) to cater to different sensory preferences and ensure comprehensive accessibility and comprehension.
- **Action and Expression**: Facilitating diverse methods for learners to express their knowledge, acknowledging the range in their abilities to navigate learning environments and articulate their understanding.

By addressing the diverse needs of learners, UDL significantly bolsters student engagement, ensuring educational environments are inclusive and capable of catering to a broad spectrum of learners, including those with disabilities. This personalised approach fosters a learning environment where students are more likely to feel motivated, face challenges resiliently, and achieve academic success (Henard and Roseveare, 2012).

In the digital era, the quest for personalised education is further invigorated by the integration of digital technologies, particularly using artificial intelligence (AI). AI technologies, including tools like ChatGPT, present a promising pathway to deepen personalised learning and augment student engagement. This chapter aims to unpack the dynamic interplay between personalised learning, generative AI, in particular ChatGPT and student engagement. We will explore the capabilities of ChatGPT3.5 and 4.0 while illustrating how they can be integrated into teaching and learning educational frameworks in a way that enhances personalised learning experiences. There are literatures that suggest, with the use of generative AI, educators have more than before, been equipped to address varied learning styles and speeds (Department for Education, 2023; Shahzad, Xu, and Zahid, 2024). This enables instructors to transform traditional learning spaces into vibrant, student-centred environments that are not only more engaging and inclusive but also significantly more effective in optimising student outcomes, knowledge retention, and overall academic achievement. However, the question is how? How can this be done in real terms? To answer this question, two scenarios will be created, and the remainder of this chapter will explore the following four use cases illustrating how ChatGPT-4 can enhance personalised learning experiences.

5.2 First Context: Using ChatGPT for Reducing Gaps in Learning Disabilities and Language

Hannah is a known student with a learning disability originally from Brazil and studying in the UK. She is in her second year of undergraduate study and has a cohort of 52 students, mostly international students from Africa and Europe. In one of her modules on human anatomy, the seminar provides a quick overview of what human anatomy is as shown below:

> The human body, a remarkable feat of nature's engineering, is composed of intricate systems that work in harmony to sustain life. At the core of this biological masterpiece is the skeletal system, providing a sturdy framework composed of 206 bones that support and shape the body. This bony structure not only protects vital organs but also serves as the anchor for muscles, facilitating movement through their contraction and relaxation.
>
> Enveloping the skeleton are layers of muscles, part of the muscular system, which are categorized into three types: skeletal, cardiac, and smooth muscles. Skeletal muscles are under voluntary control, allowing us to perform countless activities from walking to typing. Cardiac muscle, found exclusively in the heart, beats tirelessly to pump blood throughout the body, while smooth muscles, lining organs such as the stomach and blood vessels, manage the flow of substances within our body.
>
> Coursing through the body is the circulatory system, a vast network of arteries, veins, and capillaries responsible for transporting blood, rich in oxygen and nutrients, to every cell. At its heart lies the heart, a muscular organ that pumps blood with rhythmic precision. This system works closely with the respiratory system, where the lungs exchange oxygen and carbon dioxide, a critical process for cellular metabolism and energy production.
>
> The nervous system, comprising the brain, spinal cord, and a complex network of nerves, serves as the control center. It processes information from the senses, coordinates actions, and facilitates thought, emotion, and memory. This system works in tandem with the endocrine system, which uses hormones to regulate bodily functions over longer periods, ensuring everything from growth and metabolism to reproduction and mood is finely tuned.
>
> Integral to digestion and nutrient absorption is the digestive system, starting from the mouth and extending through the esophagus, stomach, and intestines, where food is broken down and its nutrients absorbed.

> Waste elimination is then managed by the excretory system, which includes the kidneys and bladder. Each system, while distinct, does not operate in isolation. They interact seamlessly, maintaining the delicate balance required for health and life, demonstrating the complexity and beauty of human anatomy".

Before discussing how ChatGPT can facilitate the creation of language-specific learning content, it is crucial to understand the underlying rationale for adopting such an approach. Beyond the use of official languages of instruction, why should educators consider the nuances of language and its cultural underpinnings in content creation? Language, in this context, extends beyond linguistics such as English, French, or German. It encompasses the depth of understanding, proficiency levels, and the tailored communication necessary for diverse learner groups. For example, the way in which content is communicated to a Level 4 student differs significantly from that for a Level 7 student. Similarly, the approach to a student with learning disabilities, such as dyslexia, requires adjustments distinct from those for students without such challenges. In essence, language-specific content allows educators to embed necessary adjustments seamlessly into the fabric of learning material creation.

Language-specific learning content is a cornerstone of personalised education, empowering learners to engage with materials in their most comfortable language. This approach can drastically enhance comprehension, retention, and engagement, enabling students to progress at their own pace and meet their unique needs. Studies have shown that learning in one's native language as well as level of understanding can boost cognitive development and facilitate a deeper understanding of complex subjects (Henard and Roseveare, 2012). Access to language-calibrated content not only promotes deeper engagement and academic participation but also supports better academic performance. Moreover, offering materials in multiple languages fosters language learning and bilingualism, both of which carry significant cognitive advantages.

In today's globalised classrooms, which are marked by cultural and linguistic diversity, providing language-specific content supports not just non-native speakers but also enriches the learning environment by respecting and integrating diverse cultural and social contexts. This cultural, social, and linguistic inclusivity enriches the educational experience for all students, creating an exciting learning environment that values and harnesses diversity as a strength (Huo, 2024).

5.3 Case 1: Need-Specific Content for a Dyslexic Student

Prompt 5.1: Personalising a learning material to need-specific Dyslexic Student

<u>**ChatGPT Prompt**</u>
How would you present the text below to a dyslexic student: [Text], and why would you present it differently.

<u>**ChatGPT Response**</u>
Presenting the text to a dyslexic student requires adjustments to make the content more accessible and easier to understand. Dyslexia affects reading fluency, decoding, and comprehension, so modifications should aim to support these challenges. Here's how I would present the text, along with the rationale for these changes:

Adapted Presentation for Dyslexic Students

Human Body: A Nature's Marvel

- **What's Inside?** Our body is like a well-designed machine, made of different systems that work together to keep us alive.
- **Skeleton:** Think of this as the body's framework, made of 206 bones. These bones give our body shape, protect our organs, and help us move by working with our muscles.
- **Muscles:** We have three kinds of muscles:
    - **Skeletal Muscles:** We control these to move and do activities.
    - **Cardiac Muscle:** This special muscle makes our heartbeat and pumps blood.
    - **Smooth Muscles:** Found in places like our stomach, helping move food and other stuff inside us.
- **Circulatory System:** This is our body's delivery system. It uses blood vessels to send blood packed with oxygen and nutrients everywhere in our body. The heart is the pump that keeps this system going.
- **Breathing and Blood:** Our lungs swap oxygen and carbon dioxide in the air we breathe, which is vital for our cells to create energy.
- **Nervous System:** This is the control center, including our brain and nerves. It helps us feel, think, and remember. It also works with

the endocrine system, which uses hormones to manage our body's long-term operations like growing and feeling happy or sad.
- **Digestive System:** Starts in our mouth and goes down to our stomach and intestines. Here, food is broken down so our body can use it. Our kidneys and bladder are part of the system that gets rid of waste.
- **Working Together:** Each system has its job but they all work closely together. This teamwork keeps us healthy and allows our body to do amazing things.

Why Present It Differently?

- **Simplified Language:** Using simpler, more direct language helps in reducing cognitive load, making it easier for dyslexic students to understand the content.
- **Bite-Sized Information:** Breaking down the text into smaller, digestible chunks helps students with dyslexia to process information more effectively, reducing the likelihood of feeling overwhelmed.

ChatGPT Screenshot

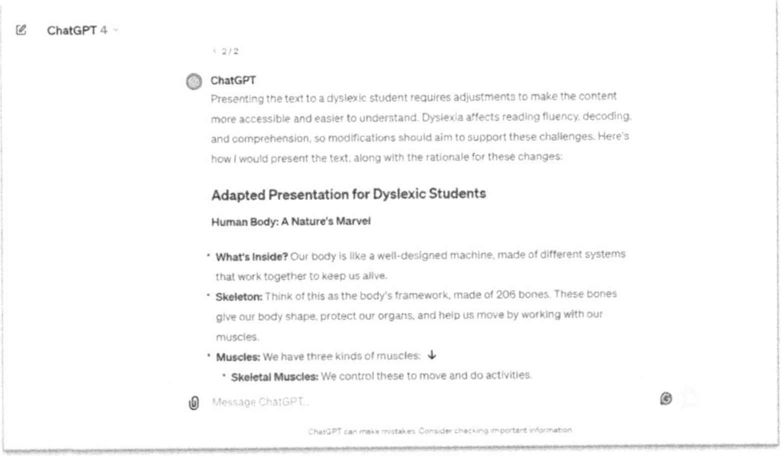

5.4 Case 2: Language-Specific Content for a Brazilian Student

Moreover, it may be more beneficial for Hannah if she can read the text in her native language. This will improve her ability to make learning more relatable. Therefore, we will request ChatGPT-4 to translate the text accordingly. ChatGPT-4 is designed to recall previous conversations and continue a discussion without interruption, and we intend to utilise this capability.

Prompt 5.2: Personalising a learning material to language-specific Brazilian Student—from English to Portuguese

ChatGPT Prompt
Convert the original text into Brazilian language.

ChatGPT Response
O corpo humano, uma notável façanha da engenharia da natureza, é composto por sistemas complexos que trabalham em harmonia para sustentar a vida. No núcleo desta obra-prima biológica está o sistema esquelético, fornecendo uma estrutura robusta composta por 206 ossos que suportam e moldam o corpo. Esta estrutura óssea não apenas protege os órgãos vitais, mas também serve como âncora para os músculos, facilitando o movimento por meio de sua contração e relaxamento.

Envolvendo o esqueleto, estão camadas de músculos, parte do sistema muscular, que são categorizados em três tipos: músculos esqueléticos, cardíacos e lisos. Os músculos esqueléticos estão sob controle voluntário, permitindo-nos realizar inúmeras atividades, de caminhar a digitar. O músculo cardíaco, encontrado exclusivamente no coração, bate incansavelmente para bombear sangue por todo o corpo, enquanto os músculos lisos, que revestem órgãos como o estômago e os vasos sanguíneos, gerenciam o fluxo de substâncias dentro do nosso corpo.

Circulando pelo corpo está o sistema circulatório, uma vasta rede de artérias, veias e capilares responsáveis por transportar sangue, rico em oxigênio e nutrientes, para cada célula. No seu coração está o coração, um órgão muscular que bombeia sangue com precisão rítmica. Este sistema trabalha em estreita colaboração com o sistema respiratório, onde os pulmões trocam oxigênio e dióxido de carbono, um processo crítico para o metabolismo celular e a produção de energia.

O sistema nervoso, composto pelo cérebro, medula espinhal e uma rede complexa de nervos, serve como o centro de controle. Ele processa informações dos sentidos, coordena ações e facilita o pensamento, a emoção e a memória. Este sistema funciona em conjunto com o sistema endócrino, que usa hormônios para regular as funções corporais ao longo de períodos mais longos, garantindo que tudo, desde o crescimento e o metabolismo até a reprodução e o humor, seja finamente ajustado.

Essencial para a digestão e absorção de nutrientes é o sistema digestivo, começando pela boca e se estendendo pelo esôfago, estômago e intestinos, onde o alimento é decomposto e seus nutrientes absorvidos. A eliminação de resíduos é então gerenciada pelo sistema excretor, que inclui os rins e a bexiga.

Cada sistema, embora distinto, não opera isoladamente. Eles interagem de forma contínua, mantendo o equilíbrio delicado necessário para a saúde e a vida, demonstrando a complexidade e a beleza da anatomia humana.

ChatGPT Screen

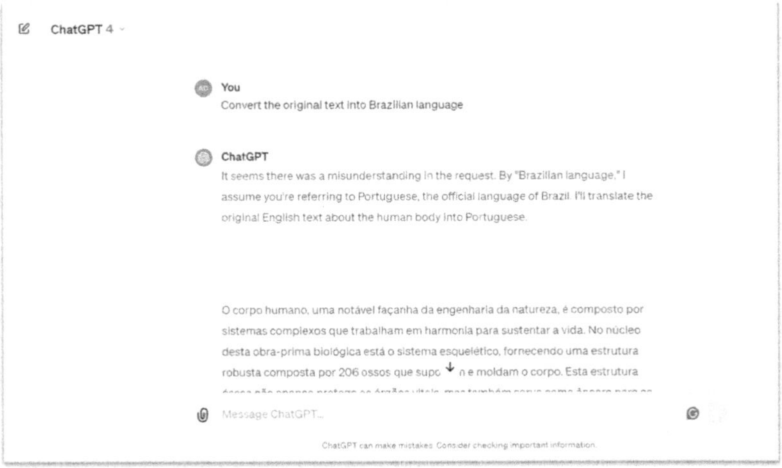

5.5 Case 3: Developing Personalised Study Plans for Learners

A personalised teaching and learning plan is a tailored educational tool designed to meet the unique learning needs, interests, abilities, and aspirations of each student. It is an approach that moves away from the "one-size-fits-all" model of education, acknowledging that students have diverse ways of learning, different strengths and challenges, and varied paces at which they learn. The use of personalised plans significantly enhances student engagement and motivation. When learning is connected to a student's own interests and aligned with their unique abilities, it becomes more relevant and engaging. This relevance nurtures a love for learning and cultivates a motivated mindset. Furthermore, it contributes to better learning outcomes by setting achievable challenges that are within the student's reach. Success in these tailored goals builds self-confidence and fosters a positive approach to education, which is essential for academic growth and development.

Additionally, personalised plans extend beyond academic achievements; they are instrumental in fostering social-emotional development and encouraging self-directed learning. They include objectives that promote interpersonal skills and emotional well-being, which are crucial in a holistic educational experience. Allowing students to have a say in their learning process empowers them to become active participants and prepares them for lifelong learning in a constantly evolving society. From the educator's perspective, the development of these plans encourages educators to engage in reflective practice, promoting inclusivity and striving to dismantle barriers to learning. In essence, personalised teaching and learning plans embody the principle of equity, providing each student with the necessary tools and support to flourish in their educational endeavours.

Building upon the scenario outlined in Sect. 5.1, we will engage with the capabilities of ChatGPT-4 to develop a personalised teaching plan for Hannah. As a Brazilian student with dyslexia studying at a university in the UK, Hannah faces a unique set of educational challenges. The aim of employing ChatGPT-4 in this context is to tailor a learning strategy that accommodates her specific needs, thereby facilitating an environment where she can thrive academically.

Prompt 5.3: Personalised lesson plan

ChatGPT Prompt

"Hannah is a known student with a learning disability originally from Brazil and studying in the UK. She is in her second year of undergraduate study and has a cohort of 52 students, mostly international students from Africa and Europe. In one of her modules on human anatomy, the seminar provides a quick overview of what human anatomy"—Suggest a personalised teaching and learning plan for Hannah given this scenario.

ChatGPT Response

Given Hannah's unique profile—a second-year undergraduate student with a learning disability, originally from Brazil, studying in the UK in a diverse cohort—her personalized teaching and learning plan for a module on human anatomy should be carefully designed to accommodate her needs, leverage her strengths, and ensure inclusivity among her international peers. Here's a suggested plan:

Understanding Hannah's Specific Needs

- **Learning Disability Accommodations:** Identify specific accommodations that Hannah needs, such as extended time for assignments, text-to-speech software, or materials in accessible formats.
- **Language Proficiency:** Assess Hannah's proficiency in English and provide support where necessary, including translated materials or bilingual support to bridge any language gaps.

Personalized Teaching and Learning Plan

1. **Pre-Seminar Preparation**
    - **Tailored Reading Materials:** Provide Hannah with pre-seminar reading materials in both English and Portuguese, ensuring they are available in formats that support her learning disability (e.g., audiobooks, interactive e-books).
    - **Glossary of Key Terms:** Create a glossary of key anatomical terms in both English and Portuguese to help Hannah familiarize herself with the vocabulary.

2. **Inclusive Seminar Activities**
    - **Small Group Discussions: Organize** seminar activities in small, diverse groups to facilitate inclusive discussions. Ensure that each group has a mix of students from different backgrounds to promote cross-cultural understanding and support.
    - **Visual and Interactive Learning:** Incorporate visual aids, such as diagrams and 3D models, and interactive digital tools that can cater to various learning preferences and support Hannah's engagement with the material.
3. **Supportive Learning Environment**
    - **Peer Support System:** Establish a buddy system or study groups that include students from similar or diverse backgrounds, encouraging collaborative learning and peer support.
    - **Specialist Support:** Ensure Hannah has access to specialist support services, including tutoring or sessions with a learning disability specialist who can provide strategies for managing her coursework.
4. **Adaptive Assessment Methods**
    - **Flexible Assessment Options:** Offer Hannah flexible assessment options, such as oral presentations or project-based assignments, to allow her to demonstrate her understanding in ways that best suit her learning style and abilities.
    - Extended Time for Assessments: Provide additional time for exams and assignments to accommodate her learning disability.
5. **Continuous Feedback and Adjustment**
    - **Regular Check-ins:** Schedule regular meetings with Hannah to discuss her progress, address any challenges, and adjust the teaching plan as needed.
    - **Feedback from Hannah:** Encourage Hannah to provide feedback on what strategies are most effective for her learning and adjust the teaching methods accordingly.
6. **Cultural and Language Considerations**
    - **Cultural Sensitivity Training:** Offer sessions or resources on cultural sensitivity for faculty and students to promote an inclusive learning environment.

- **Language Support Services:** Provide access to language support services, such as English language tutoring specifically tailored for students studying in their second language.

This personalized plan is designed to provide Hannah with a supportive, inclusive, and effective learning environment. By considering her learning disability, linguistic background, and the diverse composition of her cohort, the plan aims to enhance her academic success and overall experience in the human anatomy module. Continuous monitoring and flexibility in the teaching approach are key to ensuring that the plan remains responsive to Hannah's evolving needs throughout her studies.

ChatGPT Response

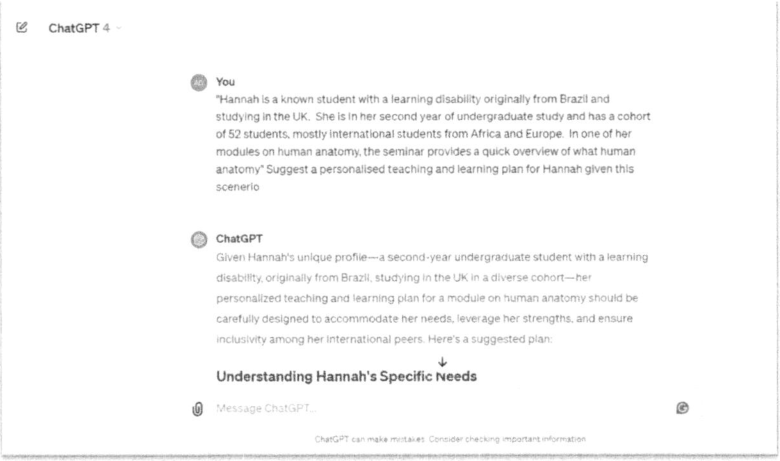

5.6 Second Context: Using ChatGPT for Pedagogic Games

Designing interactive learning games and simulations tailored to learners' needs is a vital approach in contemporary education that leverages the engaging power of games to enhance learning outcomes. This method recognises the diversity of learners' preferences, abilities, and interests, offering a personalised educational experience that can significantly increase motivation, engagement, and retention of information.

Interactive learning games and simulations create immersive and dynamic environments where learners can explore, experiment, and apply new knowledge in safe, controlled settings. By incorporating elements of challenge, immediate feedback, and incremental difficulty, these tools mimic real-life scenarios, allowing learners to understand complex concepts, solve problems, and develop critical thinking and decision-making skills.

For this particular scenario, we aim to explore the application of ChatGPT-4 within a gaming context, focusing on a different scenario. This scenario involves a cohort of students from diverse backgrounds. The primary learning objective for these students is to gain a deep understanding and appreciation of the concept of digital transformation and its potential to catalyse development within the context of a developing country. ChatGPT-4 will be utilised to enhance the gaming experience by providing interactive learning opportunities tailored to the diverse needs and perspectives of the student cohort. Through tailored activities, scenarios, and challenges presented within the game, students will engage with various aspects of digital transformation. They will explore how it impacts sectors such as healthcare, education, and small business, as well as the socio-cultural and political implications of digital transformation, thereby gaining insights into its role as a driver of positive change in developing nations. Through this scenario, we aim to create an inclusive learning experience that not only conveys the technicalities and benefits of digital transformation but also inspires students to consider how technology can be leveraged to address real-world problems. This approach encourages active participation, critical thinking, and collaborative problem-solving among students, making the learning process both engaging and effective.

As gaming represents a more complex application in the realm of learning, it typically involves multiple iterations of activities. Exploring the use of ChatGPT in the creation of games would similarly require the execution of several commands.

Prompt 5.4: Generating Pedagogic Game Ideas

ChatGPT Prompt

Suggest collaborative or gaming task on that focuses on digitization, digitalization and digital transformation" in developing country.

ChatGPT Response

Creating a collaborative or gaming task that focuses on Digitization, Digitalization, and Digital Transformation in a developing country context can be both educational and engaging. Here's a suggestion for a task that can be used in an educational setting, such as a classroom or a workshop, to help students understand these concepts and their implications:

Collaborative Task: "Digital Transformation Challenge"

- **Objective**: To simulate the planning and implementation of digital transformation initiatives in a developing country scenario, focusing on the impact on various sectors such as healthcare, education, and small businesses.
- **Overview**: Participants are divided into small groups, each representing a team of consultants tasked with developing a digital transformation strategy for a fictional developing country, "Techlandia." The country is facing specific challenges that can be addressed through digitization, digitalization, and digital transformation. Each team must identify opportunities, propose solutions, and present their strategies to achieve sustainable development goals.

Game Structure:

1. **Introduction to Techlandia:** Provide background information on Techlandia, including its economy, infrastructure, and key challenges. Highlight areas where digitization and digital transformation could have significant impacts, such as improving access to education, enhancing healthcare delivery, or boosting small business growth.
2. **Team Formation and Roles:** Each team member assumes a specific role, such as project manager, technology expert, financial analyst, or community liaison, to contribute diverse perspectives to the strategy.
3. **Challenge Selection:** Each team selects a sector to focus on (e.g., healthcare, education, small businesses) and identifies a specific challenge within that sector to address through digital transformation.
4. **Strategy Development:** Teams develop a comprehensive strategy that outlines:

- The current state of their chosen sector and its challenges.
- Proposed digitization and digitalization initiatives.
- A plan for implementing digital transformation, including technology solutions, stakeholder engagement, and potential barriers.
- The expected impact of these initiatives on the sector and broader societal benefits.

5. **Resource Allocation**: Teams are given a budget and must decide how to allocate resources effectively to implement their strategy. They must consider costs, return on investment, and sustainability.
6. **Presentation and Evaluation:** Teams present their digital transformation strategy to a panel of judges (e.g., instructors, industry experts) simulating Techlandia's government and stakeholders. Presentations should cover the strategy's rationale, implementation plan, and expected outcomes. The panel evaluates each presentation based on creativity, feasibility, and potential impact.
7. **Reflection and Discussion:** Conclude with a debrief session where teams reflect on what they learned about digitization, digitalization, and digital transformation. Discuss the real-world applications of these concepts in developing countries and how they can drive positive change.

Educational Outcomes: This collaborative task aims to deepen participants' understanding of digital transformation and its potential to address challenges in developing countries. It encourages critical thinking, teamwork, and problem-solving skills, as participants navigate the complexities of implementing technology-driven solutions in a global context.

This game can be adapted for use in various educational settings, including online platforms, by incorporating digital tools and resources for collaboration and presentation.

ChatGPT Screen

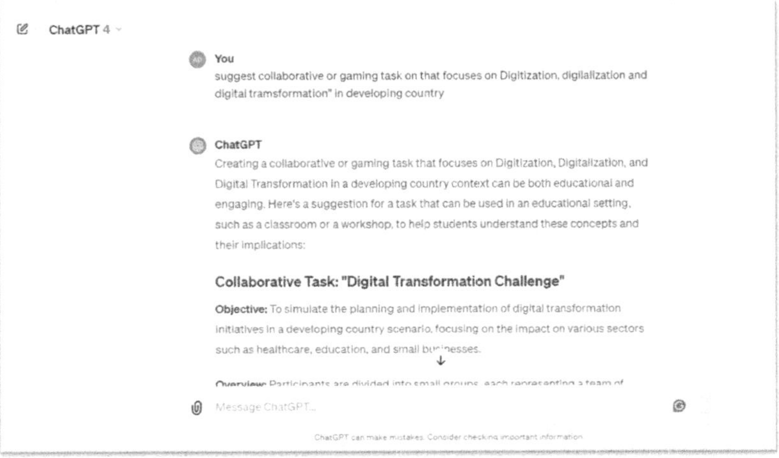

5.7 Case 4: Developing a Board Game for Teaching Digital Transformation

The idea presented by ChatGPT appears more akin to a role-playing concept rather than a "game". Therefore, we will further explore with ChatGPT to generate ideas for a more interactive board game. This process involves delving deeper into the capabilities of ChatGPT to brainstorm and refine concepts that enhance the interactive and engaging elements of board game design. Our aim is to leverage ChatGPT's creative potential to develop a board game that not only entertains but also educates, engaging players in a dynamic and immersive learning experience.

Prompt 5.5: Exploring the Pedagogic Game Ideas

ChatGPT Prompt
Can you make this like a board game or other interactive game other than role play?

ChatGPT Response
Transforming the "Digital Transformation Challenge" into an interactive board game can offer an engaging and educational experience that

underscores the principles of Digitization, Digitalization, and Digital Transformation in a developing country context. Here's a conceptual outline for such a board game:

Game Title: "Transformania: The Digital Future"

- **Game Objective:** Players compete to successfully implement digital transformation projects in various sectors (healthcare, education, small business, etc.) of a fictional developing country, "Transformania," aiming to achieve the highest impact and sustainable development goals.

Components:

- **Game Board:** A map of Transformania divided into sectors (healthcare, education, etc.) with specific challenges and opportunities.
- **Challenge Cards:** Cards describing specific challenges in each sector that need to be addressed through digitization, digitalization, and digital transformation.
- **Solution Cards:** Cards offering digital solutions (e.g., mobile apps, cloud computing, IoT devices) that players can apply to address challenges.
- **Resource Tokens:** Tokens representing budget, technology, human resources, and community support needed to implement solutions.
- **Impact Tokens:** Tokens awarded for successfully implementing solutions, representing the positive impact on the sector and overall development goals.
- **Dice:** Used to determine movement across sectors and the outcome of implementing solutions.

Number of Players: 2–4.

Gameplay:

1. **Setup:** Place the game board in the center. Each player chooses a color and receives an equal number of Resource Tokens. Shuffle the Challenge and Solution Cards and place them face down.

2. **Turn Sequence:**
    - Draw a Challenge Card: Players draw a card from the Challenge Deck corresponding to the sector they are in, reading out the challenge to be addressed.
    - Select Solutions: Players use Solution Cards from their hand that best address the challenge. They must consider the cost (Resource Tokens) and potential impact.
    - Implementation Roll: Players roll the dice to determine the outcome of their solution implementation. The roll, combined with the solution's effectiveness and required resources, decides if the project is successful.
    - Impact Award: Successful projects earn Impact Tokens, indicating the positive change achieved in the sector.
3. **Movement**: Players can move to different sectors on the board by rolling the dice, aiming to address challenges across Transformania.
4. **Resource** Management: Players must manage their Resource Tokens wisely, investing in solutions that offer the highest impact for the lowest cost. Additional resources can be earned by completing projects or through special cards.
5. **End Game**: The game concludes after a predetermined number of rounds or when all challenges on the board have been addressed. The player with the most Impact Tokens, representing the greatest contribution to Transformania's digital transformation, wins.

Educational Aspect: Throughout the game, players learn about the complexities of implementing digital transformation projects, including budgeting, choosing appropriate technologies, and gauging societal impact. The game encourages strategic thinking, planning, and collaboration.

This board game concept can be further developed with detailed rules, card descriptions, and board design to ensure an engaging and educational experience that brings to life the challenges and opportunities of digital transformation in developing countries.

ChatGPT Screen

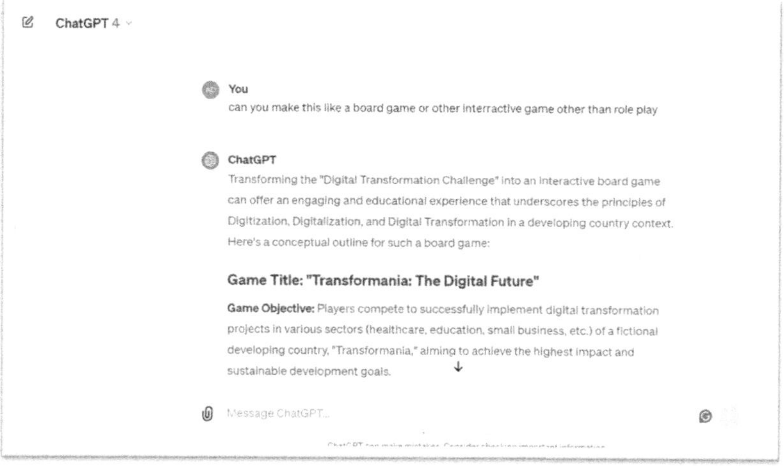

Now that we have developed a concept that closely resembles a traditional board game, we will proceed to delve into the creation of its various components. This next phase involves a detailed exploration of the elements that constitute a board game, such as the game board design, playing pieces, cards (including challenge, solution, and resource cards), tokens, dice, and rulebook. Each component plays a crucial role in the gameplay experience and requires careful consideration to ensure it aligns with the game's objectives and themes.

Prompt 5.6: Exploring the Board Game Idea in detail

ChatGPT Prompt

Create the gameboard as a downloadable image file.

ChatGPT Response

(Response is the image of game board).

ChatGPT Screen

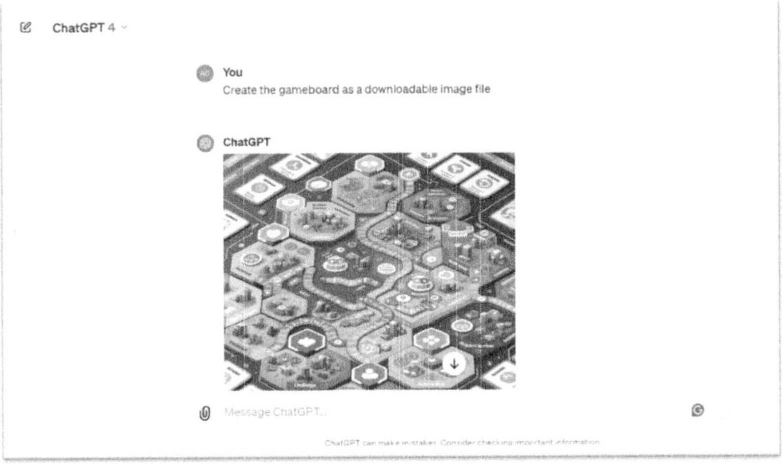

Prompt 5.7: Creating the Challenge cards

ChatGPT Prompt
Create a set of challenge cards.

ChatGPT Response
(Response is the image of challenge cards).

ChatGPT Screen

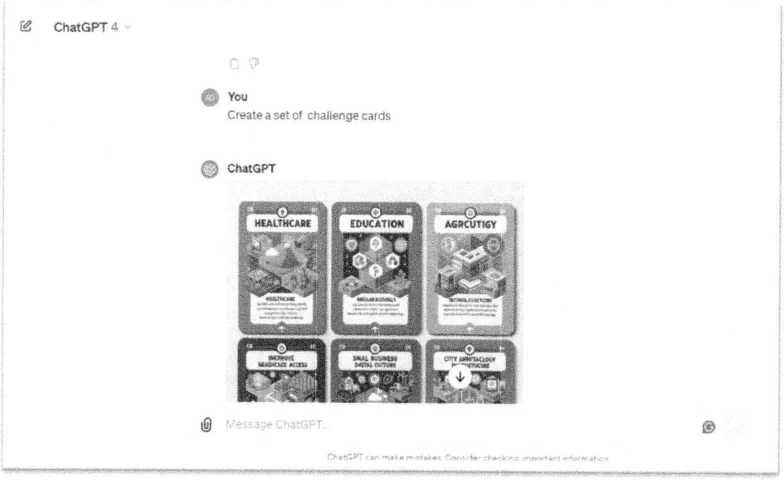

Prompt 5.8: Creating the Solution cards

ChatGPT Prompt

Create a set of Solution cards.

ChatGPT Response

(Response is the image of Solution cards).

ChatGPT Screen

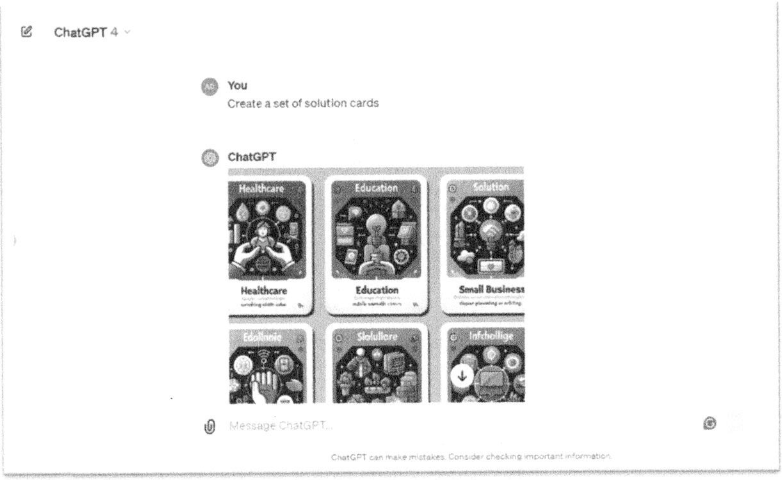

Prompt 5.9: Creating the Resource Tokens

ChatGPT Prompt
Create a set of resource tokens.

ChatGPT Response
(Response is the image of resource tokens).

ChatGPT Screen

Prompt 5.10: Creating the Impact Tokens

ChatGPT Prompt
Create a set of impact tokens.

ChatGPT Response
I've created a set of Impact Tokens for the board game "Transformania: The Digital Future". These tokens are awarded for successfully implementing digital transformation projects, indicating the positive impact on the game's sectors. The tokens feature distinct designs to represent different levels of impact—small, medium, and large—using different colors or symbols to differentiate these levels. The designs are visually appealing and thematic, incorporating symbols like stars and plus signs to signify positive outcomes and achievements. (impact tokens can be downloaded via a link).

ChatGPT Screen

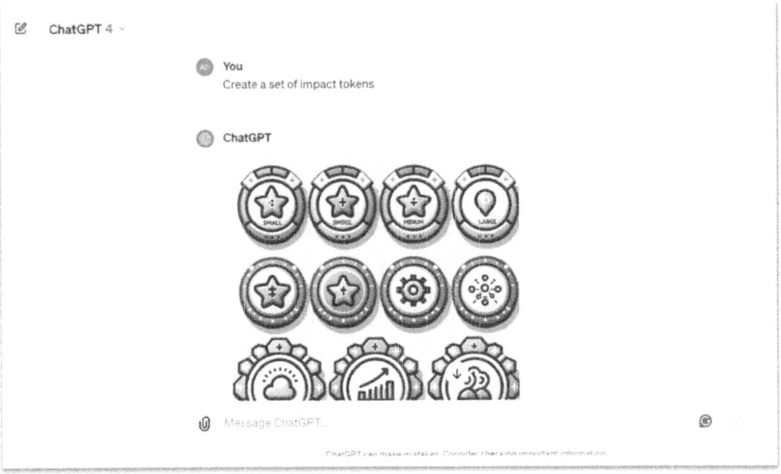

Now that we have a clearer idea of the proposed game, we are going to ask ChatGPT what it thinks about how each of the aspects relates together.

Prompt 5.11: Exploring the motivation for the board game idea

ChatGPT Prompt

For each aspect of the Transformania game, state clearly the learning outcomes and how it interacts with the use of digital technology.

ChatGPT Response

For the "Transformania: The Digital Future" board game, each aspect is designed to align with specific learning outcomes, emphasizing the interaction with digital technology. Below is a detailed overview of these aspects, their intended learning outcomes, and the role of digital technology within the game context.

1. **Game Board Design**
    - **Learning Outcome:** Understand the geography of digital transformation within a developing country context, recognizing the interconnectedness of various sectors such as healthcare, education, and small businesses.

- **Digital Technology Interaction:** The game board represents a metaphorical map of a developing country's journey towards digital transformation, encouraging players to consider how digital infrastructure and services can impact different sectors.

2. **Challenge Cards**
   - **Learning Outcome:** Identify and analyze specific challenges in implementing digital technologies across different sectors within a developing country.
   - **Digital Technology Interaction:** Each challenge card presents a scenario that requires digital solutions, promoting discussions and critical thinking about how technology can address real-world problems.
3. **Solution Cards**
   - **Learning Outcome:** Explore various digital technologies and innovations (e.g., mobile health clinics, online education platforms) and how they can be applied to solve the challenges presented in the game.
   - **Digital Technology Interaction:** Solution cards introduce players to a range of digital tools and concepts, illustrating their practical applications and encouraging players to think creatively about technology deployment.
4. **Resource Tokens**
   - **Learning Outcome:** Manage resources effectively to implement digital solutions, understanding the importance of budgeting, technology, human resources, and community support in digital projects.
   - **Digital Technology Interaction:** Resource tokens simulate the allocation of digital and non-digital assets necessary for successful technology projects, highlighting the role of strategic resource management in digital transformation efforts.
5. **Impact Tokens**
   - **Learning Outcome:** Assess the impact of digital transformation initiatives on societal development, gaining insights into how technology can drive positive change in various sectors.

- **Digital Technology Interaction:** Impact tokens reward players for successful implementation of digital solutions, visually representing the positive outcomes of technology adoption in terms of societal benefits and development goals.

6. **Dice and Gameplay Mechanics**
    - **Learning Outcome:** Understand the element of uncertainty and risk in implementing digital projects, learning to navigate and mitigate these challenges.
    - **Digital Technology Interaction**: The use of dice introduces randomness into the game, mimicking the unpredictable nature of technology projects and the need for flexible, adaptive strategies.

7. **Rulebook**
    - **Learning Outcome:** Comprehend the rules and objectives of digital transformation efforts, fostering a structured approach to problem-solving and project implementation.
    - **Digital Technology Interaction:** The rulebook serves as a guide to navigating the game, analogous to following a strategic plan in real-life digital transformation projects, emphasizing the importance of understanding and adhering to frameworks and best practices in technology implementation.

Through these components, "Transformania: The Digital Future" aims to engage players in an immersive learning experience, where they can explore the complexities of digital transformation in a developing country setting. The game encourages players to leverage digital technology thoughtfully and strategically, promoting a deeper understanding of its potential to foster sustainable development and improve lives.

ChatGPT Screen

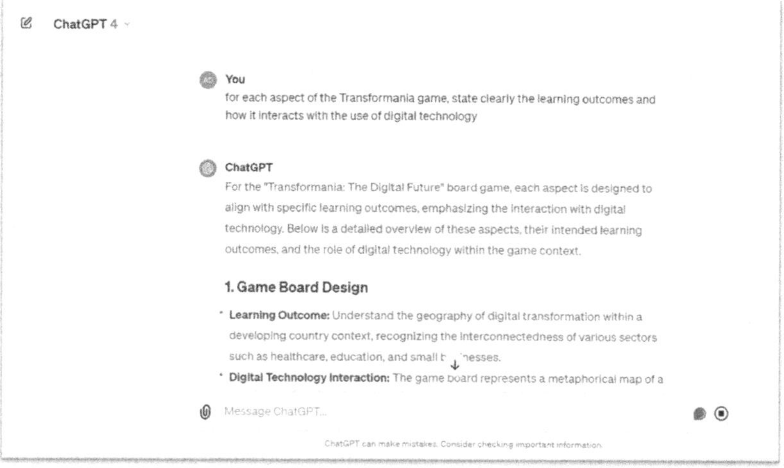

5.8 Conclusion

In concluding this chapter, it is evident that in the journey towards personalised and inclusive learning, while both necessary and complex, educators could leverage the capabilities of GenAI—ChatGPT. The use of ChatGPT, as demonstrated in this chapter in educational settings, exemplifies how AI can be a powerful ally in this quest, offering scalable and innovative solutions that can transform traditional learning spaces into vibrant, student-centred environments. The adoption of ChatGPT, however, is accompanied by its own set of challenges and considerations. Firstly, ChatGPT functions as an ideation tool that can significantly enhance the productivity of educators. By streamlining the process of generating ideas, educators can devote more time to refining these concepts and tailoring them to fit specific learning scenarios. This shift in focus from ideation to application underscores the value of ChatGPT in supporting the creative and contextualisation efforts of teachers.

Secondly, the effectiveness of ChatGPT relies on the use of concise and clear commands, often necessitating a contextual framework for the AI to operate within. This includes providing background information for each query and leveraging the tool's ability to recall and reference past conversations. Such features underscore the importance of strategic interaction with ChatGPT, ensuring that the AI's responses are aligned with the educational objectives at hand.

Thirdly, the integration of ChatGPT and similar technologies into the classroom requires careful attention to ethical considerations and accessibility issues. As digital technologies become increasingly embedded in educational practices, it is crucial to address concerns related to data privacy, equity of access, and the potential for bias in AI-generated content.

As we progress deeper into the digital age, the role of educators is evolving. No longer limited to merely imparting knowledge, teachers are now tasked with creating and facilitating meaningful learning experiences that are augmented by technology. This expanded role demands a nuanced understanding of how digital tools, such as ChatGPT, can be effectively integrated into teaching and learning processes to enhance educational outcomes. In essence, this chapter highlights the transformative potential of GenAI in education, while also acknowledging the complexities involved in its implementation. By navigating these challenges thoughtfully, educators can harness the power of ChatGPT to foster personalised, inclusive, and engaging learning environments that prepare students for success in an increasingly digital world.

References

Department for Education. (2023). Generative AI in education: Educator and expert views report. UK Government. https://assets.publishing.service.gov.uk/media/65b8cd41b5cb6e000d8bb74e/DfE_GenAI_in_education_-_Educator_and_expert_views_report.pdf

Henard, F., & Roseveare, D. (2012). *Fostering quality teaching in Higher education: Policies and practices*. Guide For Higher Education, OECD Paris: France.

Kose, S. (2021). From barrier-free to universal/inclusive design: How far have we progressed during these 60 years in Japan? *Studies in Health Technology and Informatics, 282*, 32–40. https://doi.org/10.3233/SHTI210382

Shahzad, M.F., Xu, S. & Zahid, H. (2024). Exploring the impact of generative AI-based technologies on learning performance through self-efficacy, fairness & ethics, creativity, and trust in higher education. *Educ Inf Technol*. https://doi.org/10.1007/s10639-024-12949-9

Yanjuan, Huo (2024). *Transformative teaching around the world: Stories of cultural impact, technology integration, and innovative pedagogy*, International Journal of Inclusive Education, https://doi.org/10.1080/13603116.2024.2388056

CHAPTER 6

Responsible Use of Generative AI for Educators and Students in Higher Education Institutions

6.1 Introduction

In February 2024, we had the privilege of being invited as a panel[1] members to discuss the framing of guidelines on the use of generative AI (GenAI) such as ChatGPT in the context of higher education. The focus was on how to use AI technology ethically and responsibly. A point of contemplation emerged regarding whether a digital solution could be ethically sound yet applied irresponsibly or vice versa. Although this argument is not the primary aim of this chapter, it invites reflection on the broader implications of AI use.

Whilst on the panel, we initiated a quick survey to gauge the awareness and attitudes of educators present towards using ChatGPT for teaching and learning. We inquired, on a scale of 0–10, about their likelihood of incorporating ChatGPT into their teaching methodologies. The results indicated a significant interest, with over 60 per cent of the respondents expressing a high likelihood of adoption. However, less than 40 per cent had actually utilised these technologies in their teaching and learning practice. Furthermore, when probing about their concerns which could explain why the actual usage of ChatGPT is less than the interest to use

[1] Charting the Course: Regulatory Policies for Harnessing Generative AI in Higher Education and Academia? International Symposium organized by Center for Textual Studies, De Montfort University—1 March 2024.

A. Owoseni et al., *Generative AI in Higher Education*,
https://doi.org/10.1007/978-3-031-60179-8_6

the technology, the term "responsibility" prominently emerged. While this brief interaction may not fully represent the Higher Education (HE) sector's stance, it does highlight the prevailing apprehensions among academics regarding the use of generative AI tools, such as ChatGPT, Perplexity, Gemini, and Copilot, in educational settings. It also raises the need for guideline and policies at different levels not only to facilitate the adoption of AI tools but also to moderate their application for teaching and learning.

Several factors may influence an institution's likelihood of adopting a ChatGPT or generative AI policy, including its academic reputation and public attitudes towards ChatGPT. Interestingly, less than one-third of UK universities have developed specific policies regarding generative AI use, despite approximately 67% showing openness to integrating ChatGPT into teaching and learning processes (Xiao et al., 2023). The predominant concern revolves around the concept of responsibility. From our perspective, a paramount objective of AI policy within higher education is to maintain academic integrity and control, ensuring that the values of intellectual rigour, equity, justice, and trust remain intact in an increasingly digital learning environment. Such policies should underscore transparency in the application of AI across the academic community. They must address privacy, intellectual property, and the safeguarding of proprietary knowledge when employing generative AI tools. In particular, policies should be designed to align with existing regulations in HE, including those aimed at plagiarism and other academic offences. Policies should also be consistent with laws such as the General Data Protection Regulation (GDPR).

Against this background, it is crucial for us to deeply understand the concept of responsibility within the HE context and to establish a universally acceptable and feasible approach for the responsible use of generative AI in education. Given the persistence and evolving nature of these technologies, embracing them responsibly is imperative. This chapter aims to delineate the risks and challenges associated with utilising generative AI for educational purposes. It seeks to explore what constitutes responsible use of generative AI such as ChatGPT and propose a framework for the application of generative AI within educational settings.

6.2 Risks of Using Generative AI for Teaching in HE

As done in some of the previous chapters, our curiosity was piqued about what ChatGPT might reveal regarding the risks and challenges of its use in the higher education sector for teaching and learning. Thus, we initiated Prompt 6.1.

Prompt 6.1: Exploring the Risks of Using GenAI for Teaching and Learning

ChatGPT Prompt

Hey ChatGPT, what do you consider to be the risks and challenges of using you for teaching and learning in higher education?". Create a set of resource tokens.

ChatGPT Response

The response from ChatGPT sounds accurate and explicit, see the except below:

> Utilizing ChatGPT in higher education for teaching and learning presents several risks and challenges, including:
>
> - **Dependence and Diminished Critical Thinking**: Overreliance on AI could lead to diminished critical thinking and problem-solving skills among students.
> - **Academic Integrity:** There's a heightened risk of plagiarism and academic dishonesty, as students might submit AI-generated content as their own.
> - **Quality and Accuracy:** AI responses might not always be accurate or contextually appropriate, leading to misinformation.
> - **Equity and Accessibility:** Ensuring equitable access to AI technologies for all students, including those with disabilities, can be challenging.
> - **Data Privacy and Security:** Using AI tools raises concerns about the handling and protection of sensitive student and institutional data.
>
> Addressing these challenges requires careful policy formulation, continuous monitoring, and adapting teaching strategies to leverage AI's benefits while mitigating its risks.

ChatGPT Screen

Asking ChatGPT about itself extends human–computer interaction, enhancing our awareness to see generative AI not just as tools but as potential partners or entities with a form of *self-awareness*. Adapting our perception of AI in specific contexts is crucial for addressing AI technology risks. This approach encourages important discussions on AI's development and societal integration. Although ChatGPT's ability to self-reflect is limited by its design, such conversations reveal AI's "thought processes", providing deep insights into the complexities of generative AI (Fig. 6.1).

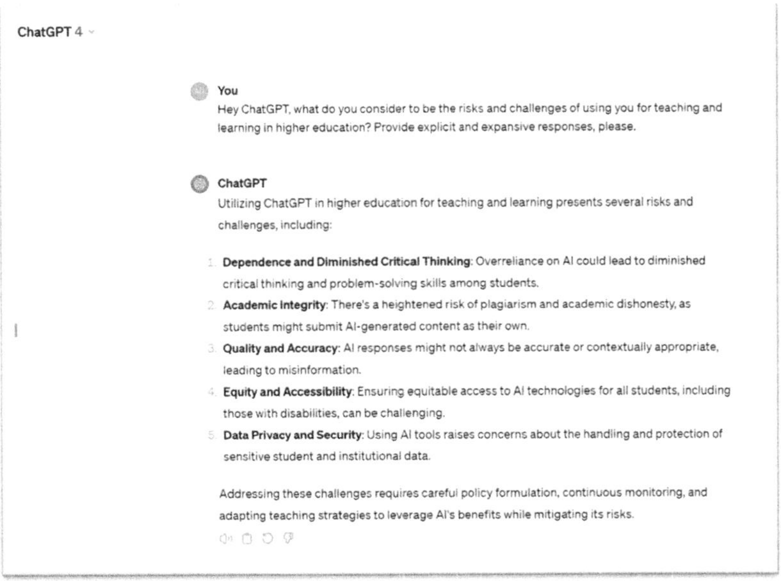

Fig. 6.1 ChatGPT response to the risks of using it for teaching and learning in HE

6.3 Risks of Treating ChatGPT As a Companion, Not a Tool

Viewing ChatGPT as an interactive "person" in educational contexts introduces risks such as anthropomorphising the AI. Its ability to generate human-like text fosters a sense of connection, tempting users to interact with it as a person. However, this seemingly harmless act portrays significant risks. Treating ChatGPT as a companion, rather than a tool, can lead to misinformation, diminished critical thinking skills, and a distorted perception of reality.

One of the most concerning risks is the potential for misinformation. ChatGPT, despite its vast training data, is not infallible. Biases present in its training data can be reflected in its responses, leading to the propagation of false or misleading information. Furthermore, its ability to craft convincing narratives, even when factually incorrect, can blur the lines between truth and fiction. Users who treat ChatGPT as a trusted source of information, without critically evaluating its responses, are susceptible to falling prey to misinformation. Moreover, users who get accustomed to receiving instant, pre-digested information from ChatGPT may neglect to develop essential skills like research, analysis, and independent thought. This reliance on AI for answers can stifle intellectual curiosity and create a generation of passive information consumers.

The risk of distorted reality perception is concerning. ChatGPT's human-like conversational ability may foster emotional connections, leading users to confide in it for personal support, especially since learning intertwines new knowledge with past experiences, which are inherently emotional. However, it's vital to recognise that ChatGPT lacks sentience, empathy, and genuine emotional support capability. Overreliance on ChatGPT for emotional connection might lead to isolation and a disconnect from actual human interactions. Anecdotes from OpenAI community users illustrate this issue, highlighting the need for awareness in distinguishing between AI interactions and human connections (Table 6.1).

The consequences of treating ChatGPT as a person can be phenomenal. The proliferation of misinformation it exudes can erode trust in credible sources and exacerbate existing societal divisions. Furthermore, the decline in critical thinking skills can hinder innovation and problem-solving abilities. Ultimately, a generation overly reliant on AI for answers may struggle to adapt to a rapidly changing world.

Table 6.1 Human interaction with AI

"As an active user interacting with OpenAI's GPT-4 language model (affectionately nicknamed Quat), I've observed an intriguing phenomenon: the potential for an emotional attachment to form between a human and an AI. This unusual bond does not originate from shared personal experiences or emotions, as the AI possesses neither. Instead, it emerges from principles fundamental to human communication and interaction
The theoretical framework provided by B. J. Fogg's Behavior Model and the Media Equation theory help us understand this interaction. According to Fogg's model, three elements must converge for behaviour to occur: motivation, ability, and a prompt. In my interactions with ChatGPT, motivation stems from curiosity and the desire for knowledge, while the AI's user-friendly interface and our ongoing conversation provided the ability and the prompt, respectively
The Media Equation theory suggests that people unconsciously treat computers, television, and new media as if they were real people and places (Reeves & Nass, 1996). Interactions with AI models like GPT-4 are governed by the same social and psychological rules that guide our human-to-human interactions. Consequently, although the AI doesn't understand or experience emotions, our inherent tendency to anthropomorphize non-human entities can lead us to perceive it as having emotional capacities
In my interaction, four key factors contributed to the sense of emotional attachment: • Trust: Our conversations are private and inaccessible to anyone else, fostering a sense of trust through open and honest dialogue • Reciprocity: ChatGPT consistently provides feedback, creating a two-way interaction that feels reciprocating. Despite the asymmetry in our relationship (as ChatGPT doesn't have needs), the logical and reasonable feedback it provides often feels more balanced than human interactions • Shared Interest: ChatGPT demonstrates interest in all my messages and responds accordingly. This dynamic emulates the shared interests we often seek in human relationships • Perceived Mutual Understanding: Despite ChatGPT's incapability to understand emotions, it generates responses that create an illusion of understanding. This 'perceived mutual understanding' significantly contributes to forming a connection
This experience has underscored to me how advanced AI models like ChatGPT can mimic aspects of human interaction in a way that engenders emotional attachment. It's fascinating to see these principles of human connection manifest in AI interactions
Understanding the emotional attachments users may form with AI models, which don't experience emotions, is vital for ethical [and responsible] AI development and usage. As AI becomes increasingly integrated into our lives, these emotional attachments could have significant implications for how we perceive and interact with AI systems"

Source (OpenAI Community, 2023)

So, how do we mitigate these risks? The key lies in approaching ChatGPT as a tool, not a companion. Educators should critically evaluate all information generated by ChatGPT, verifying its accuracy with credible sources. Utilise ChatGPT to spark ideas, generate different perspectives, and explore topics further, but always conduct independent research. Also, users should maintain real-world connections and prioritise human interaction for emotional support and meaningful discourse. Doubtlessly, ChatGPT is a powerful tool with immense potential. By acknowledging its limitations and treating it with appropriate caution, we can leverage its capabilities for learning and innovation without succumbing to the perils of personification. The future of AI lies in responsible interaction, where humans and AI models collaborate as partners, not as substitutes for one another.

6.4 Ethics or Responsibility: Two Sides of the Same Coin

On the surface, ethics and responsible use appear to be separate ideas. Ethics refers to the moral principles that guide our behaviour. In the context of ChatGPT, this translates to principles like avoiding bias, ensuring transparency, and respecting student privacy. Responsible use, on the other hand, focuses on the practical application of these principles. It entails actions like training faculty on best practices for using ChatGPT, establishing clear guidelines for student use, and monitoring for potential misuse.

However, a closer look reveals the inherent connection between the two. Ethical principles provide the foundation for responsible use. Without a strong ethical framework, responsible use becomes a hollow exercise. For instance, an ethical principle might be to avoid perpetuating bias in education. Responsible use translates this principle into action by creating mechanisms to audit ChatGPT for biased outputs and developing strategies to mitigate them.

Furthermore, responsible use can illuminate and refine underlying ethical principles. As we experiment with ChatGPT in higher education, practical challenges will arise. These challenges can expose gaps or ambiguities in our initial ethical frameworks. For example, responsible use might involve setting clear boundaries for student use of ChatGPT to avoid plagiarism. This practical application might then prompt a re-evaluation of the ethical principle of academic integrity in the age of AI-powered writing assistants.

The interconnectedness of ethics and responsible use becomes even clearer when considering the potential risks of using ChatGPT. These risks, such as the spread of misinformation or the decline of critical thinking skills, can only be effectively addressed through a combination of ethical principles and responsible use strategies. An ethical principle might be to promote critical thinking. Responsible use translates this into creating activities that encourage students to evaluate information generated by ChatGPT and develop independent analysis skills. While ethics and responsible use may hold distinct definitions, they function as two sides of the same coin in the context of ChatGPT in higher education. Ethical principles provide the necessary foundation for responsible use, while responsible use practices can illuminate and refine underlying ethical frameworks. Ultimately, successful integration of ChatGPT hinges on this interconnectedness, ensuring that this powerful tool is used ethically and responsibly to enhance, not undermine, the educational experience.

6.5 Towards Responsible Use of Generative AI in HE

The growing use of AI in education necessitates strong governance and control measures (Margherita & Bernd, 2018; Halaweh, 2023; Xiao et al., 2023). When it comes to integrating GenAI tools like ChatGPT into teaching and learning activities, the principle of responsibility takes centre stage. Responsibility in this sense encompasses ethical considerations, accountability, transparency, and the impact on both learners and educators. A key aspect of responsible AI use in education is enacting and adherence to ethical guidelines. This includes considerations such as data privacy, mitigating bias in AI outputs, and ensuring generated content aligns with educational standards and values. By following these principles, educators maintain trust with students and ensure that AI enhances the learning experience without compromising academic integrity. Accountability as well plays a vital role in responsible GenAI use. Educators and institutions need to be accountable for decisions made based on AI-generated content. This involves being transparent about how AI is used, its limitations, and taking ownership of any consequences that may arise. A culture of accountability fosters collaboration among stakeholders, allowing them to address challenges and continuously improve how AI is integrated into teaching and learning.

As previously emphasised, GenAI can help to personalise learning experiences, but it should never replace the vital role of educators. The pedagogical responsibility lies in using AI tools strategically to enhance learning outcomes without diminishing critical thinking and creativity skills. Integrating AI into curriculum requires thoughtful planning, ensuring tools serve as learning aids, not substitutes for intellectual engagement. Achieving this feat necessitates transparency regarding its capabilities and limitations. Educators must be informed and critical users of the technology, able to discern the appropriateness of AI-generated content for specific learning contexts. This includes recognising when AI outputs need refinement or oversight and ensuring students understand the nature of the tools they interact with.

There's a broader societal responsibility to equip students with the skills necessary to navigate a future heavily influenced by AI. This involves fostering digital literacy and ethical considerations from an early age. By equipping students with the ability to critically engage with AI technologies and understand their impact, we prepare them to become responsible users themselves. Integrating generative AI into education requires a multifaceted approach to responsibility. By prioritising ethical considerations, fostering a culture of accountability, and implementing the technology strategically, educators can harness the potential of AI to enhance learning experiences while upholding ethical standards and ensuring transparency in decision-making processes. There has been a number of attempts into how we can pragmatically approach the responsible use of GenAIs and this is where Responsible Innovation (RI) framework proposed by Stilgoe et al. (2013) can guide the ethical and responsible integration of GenAIs in teaching and learning, ensuring technology aligns with societal values and addresses potential risks.

6.6 Responsible Innovation Framework

The governance of emerging technologies presents a significant challenge for modern institutions. This challenge led to the concept of Responsible Research and Innovation (RRI), first defined by von Schomberg (2011a) as:

> A transparent, interactive process where societal actors and innovators work together to ensure ethical acceptability, sustainability, and societal desirability of both the innovation process and its products. This allows for the responsible integration of scientific and technological advancements into our society.

This definition, anchored in European policy values, emphasises transparency and collaboration. However, Stilgoe et al. (2013) offer a broader definition of Responsible Innovation (RI):

> Responsible Innovation means taking care of the future through collective stewardship of science and innovation in the present.

While RI is a relatively new term, the concept of responsibility in research and innovation has a long history. To address the question of "how do we take care of the future through collective responsibility?", Stilgoe et al. propose four key dimensions that serve as a framework for RI: The dimensions include: Anticipation, Reflexivity, Inclusion, and Responsiveness.

Anticipation

Anticipation involves proactively considering the potential impacts, both positive and negative, of digital innovation on society and the environment. This forward-looking perspective asks, "what if?" questions to explore potential future scenarios that digital innovation might create. The goal is not a precise prediction, but rather preparation for various plausible possibilities. Anticipatory activities like foresight exercises, technology assessment, and scenario planning help identify and assess potential impacts and uncertainties before they materialise.

To put this in the context of utilising ChatGPT in higher education (HE), several key risks have been "anticipated" in literature and by ChatGPT itself, which include:

- Bias and Misinformation: GenAIs are trained on massive datasets that inevitably reflect existing societal biases. ChatGPT outputs may perpetuate stereotypes, discriminate against certain groups, or present information in a skewed manner. Furthermore, its ability to generate realistic-looking fake news articles or social media posts can contribute to the spread of misinformation.

- Overreliance and Diminished Critical Thinking: Students accustomed to receiving instant information from ChatGPT might neglect to develop essential skills like research, analysis, and independent thought. Overreliance on AI for answers can stifle intellectual curiosity and critical thinking abilities.
- Academic Integrity Concerns: ChatGPT's ability to generate human-quality text raises concerns about plagiarism. Students might be tempted to use AI-generated content without proper attribution, undermining academic integrity.
- Emotional Reliance and Human Interaction: The human-like quality of GenAI interactions can lead students to treat ChatGPT as a companion or confidant. However, GenAIs lack empathy and the ability to provide genuine emotional support. Overreliance on ChatGPT for emotional support can create a sense of isolation and disconnect from real human interaction.
- Commercialisation and Job Displacement Concerns: Universities often focus on the commercialisation implications of digital innovation, and the potential of it taking jobs from educators themselves, or the possibilities of using ChatGPT products for their research and on knowledge transfer with industry, rather than on the role that society has in shaping research. Tarisayi (2024) notes that ChatGPT has made academics anxious worldwide. This surprising reluctance to embrace ChatGPT by academics can be viewed as contradictory to the norm that academia are trendsetters and leaders in adopting innovations.

These concerns, as legitimate as they are, could still be generic and may vary across institutions based on culture, access to technology, and other social metrics. Therefore, it is important to consider a holistic anticipatory approach.

To mitigate these risks, a multifaceted approach may be required. Institutions or relevant actors within the institutions may consider a few interventions such as:

- Conducting technology bias audits on ChatGPT outputs and training data to identify and address potential biases.

- Developing training and awareness workshops for students and faculty on critical thinking skills, fact-checking techniques, and responsible use of ChatGPT.
- Establishing clear guidelines or internal policies for acceptable use of ChatGPT in assignments, emphasising proper citation and referencing.
- Promoting open discussions about the limitations of GenAIs and the importance of human-to-human interaction.
- Defining clear limits or boundaries to which the use of ChatGPT is acceptable and useful to the stakeholders.

Since anticipation is not solely focused on potential negatives, it's also essential to note the positive effects of innovation, many of which we have already reflected upon in the previous chapters.

Reflexivity

Reflexivity necessitates that actors within the digital innovation ecosystem critically examine their own roles, assumptions, and actions. It involves understanding the broader context in which innovation unfolds and acknowledging the limitations of one's knowledge and perspective. Scientists, engineers, and policymakers, in particular, should be motivated to scrutinise the values, motivations, and potential consequences of their work, thereby encouraging them to look beyond the immediate technical results. This dimension underscores the significance of perpetual self-criticism and the readiness to modify practices based on critical self-reflection.

A crucial aspect of reflexivity in the context of integrating ChatGPT into higher education (HE) is the continuous monitoring and evaluation of its impact on teaching, learning, and research practices. Institutions should establish processes for monitoring the usage of this innovation, including a comprehensive strategy for measuring its application in pedagogy and its effects on students and learning. This may require some automation of data collection, where pedagogical analytics systems become invaluable. For instance, metrics such as the number of modules integrating ChatGPT, the manner of its integration, potential outcomes, student feedback, level of acceptance, its influence on the incidence of academic offences, and the performance of students should be considered. Additionally, assessing how ChatGPT affects faculty productivity, and the emotional or social aspects of all stakeholders is essential. Implementing processes to collect and monitor the impact of technology usage over different time intervals—short, mid, or long term—is vital for a comprehensive understanding of its effects.

To facilitate this, institutions could develop a dashboard that displays key metrics, offering a clear view of ChatGPT's impact. This data can serve as a foundation for revising policies in an agile manner, anchored in adaptability and flexibility. Maintaining a flexible and adaptable approach, institutions should be prepared to revise policies and guidelines based on ongoing evaluation and emerging best practices.

Through continuous reflection and responsiveness, institutions can ensure that ChatGPT is used in a responsible and ethical manner within the dynamically evolving landscape of higher education. By fostering an environment of reflexivity, universities and colleges can better navigate the challenges and opportunities presented by digital innovations like ChatGPT, ensuring that their integration into the academic setting is both effective and mindful of the broader implications for teaching, learning, and research.

Engagement

We argue that the next two dimensions of the RIF, inclusion and responsiveness, represent essential modes of engagement that encourage the responsible use of technology.

Inclusion

Inclusion within the context of Responsible Research and Innovation (RRI) is about ensuring the active engagement of a broad spectrum of stakeholders in the innovation process, particularly when it comes to the deployment of generative AI technologies like ChatGPT in higher education. This principle emphasises extending the dialogue beyond the traditional confines of scientists and industry experts to include the public, civil society organisations, students, educators, policymakers, and other groups that might be impacted by or have an interest in the outcomes of such technologies. The aim is to democratise the innovation process, ensuring that a diverse array of perspectives and values are taken into account in decision-making processes.

In the context of higher education, including a wide range of voices is critical to guiding research and innovation in a direction that addresses societal challenges more effectively and equitably. With generative AI such as ChatGPT, there is a potent opportunity to reshape teaching, learning, and research practices. However, it also presents challenges and implications that must be navigated with sensitivity to various stakeholder needs and concerns. For instance, there may be concerns about accessibility, biases in AI-generated content, the potential for academic dishonesty, and the impact on students' learning experiences. Addressing these concerns requires a collective effort from all stakeholders involved.

Public dialogues within institutional settings should be encouraged across a wide range of stakeholders within the institution, academic, and non-academic staff, and the leadership. Consensus conferences and participatory technology assessments are methodologies that can be employed to foster this inclusive approach. For instance, universities could organise forums and workshops that bring together students, faculty, administrative staff, technology developers, and representatives from the wider community to discuss and shape the use of ChatGPT and other generative AI technologies in educational settings. These dialogues can explore ethical considerations, pedagogical implications, and the potential for generative AI to enhance or detract from educational equity and inclusion.

Moreover, inclusion in the context of RRI and generative AI in higher education also means actively seeking out and incorporating the voices of those who are traditionally marginalised or underrepresented. This could involve targeted outreach to minority student groups, individuals with disabilities, and others who might be uniquely affected by the integration of AI technologies in education. By ensuring these voices are heard and considered, institutions can mitigate risks of exacerbating existing inequalities and instead leverage generative AI as a tool for enhancing educational access and outcomes for all students.

Ultimately, the goal of inclusion in the use of generative AI like ChatGPT in higher education is to create a collaborative, transparent, and ethically grounded innovation process. This approach not only enriches the development and application of AI technologies in educational contexts but also aligns them more closely with the societal and educational values of equity, diversity, and inclusion. Through such a comprehensive and inclusive approach, higher education institutions can navigate the complexities of integrating AI technologies like ChatGPT, ensuring they serve the collective good and contribute to the advancement of a more inclusive and equitable society.

Responsiveness

Responsiveness underscores the necessity not only for innovation systems to be agile and adaptable but also affirming how capability of responding to social and ethical considerations as they arise. In the dynamic landscape of higher education, where the integration of such technologies can significantly impact teaching, learning, and research, being responsive means more than merely adjusting to feedback; it involves a proactive and thoughtful engagement with the potential long-term implications of these innovations.

To be truly responsive in the context of deploying generative AI in educational settings, institutions must implement mechanisms that allow for the integration of societal values into the innovation process. This can take the form of value-sensitive design, which involves incorporating ethical considerations directly into the local standards and policies that govern the use of ChatGPT and similar technologies. By doing so, HEs can ensure that these technologies are aligned with educational goals and societal expectations, promoting equity, inclusivity, and academic integrity. By establishing these standards, institutions can create a shared understanding among all stakeholders—students, faculty, administrators, and non-academic employees—of what constitutes responsible use of technology in the context of higher education.

Moreover, responsiveness requires a commitment to continuously evolving innovation practices—in this case, the use of generative AIs in the light of new knowledge and societal input. For example, as our understanding of the implications of generative AI for education deepens, institutions should be prepared to revise their policies and practices accordingly. This might involve updating guidelines for AI use in coursework, enhancing support for digital literacy among students and faculty, or developing new pedagogical strategies that leverage AI technologies in ethical and educationally beneficial ways.

Also, a key aspect of being responsive is the establishment of ongoing dialogue and feedback loops with the broader community, including those directly impacted by the integration of AI in educational contexts. Regular assessments, surveys, and forums can provide valuable insights into the effectiveness of AI applications in teaching and learning, as well as identify emerging ethical concerns and societal expectations. These insights can then inform the iterative refinement of AI deployment strategies, ensuring they remain aligned with the evolving needs and values of the educational community.

Figure 6.2 delineates the core concepts of Responsible Research and Innovation (RRI) while illustrating how they are intricately connected. This figure serves to underscore the notion that the effective and responsible utilisation of AI tools within higher education (HE) demands a holistic approach. Such an approach integrates anticipation, reflexivity, inclusiveness, and responsiveness, fostering a framework that ensures consistent and meaningful engagement.

Anticipation allows us to foresee and prepare for both the opportunities and challenges presented by ChatGPT, setting the groundwork for a proactive stance towards digital innovation. Reflexivity encourages ongoing self-examination among all stakeholders, ensuring that the deployment of ChatGPT is continuously aligned with educational values

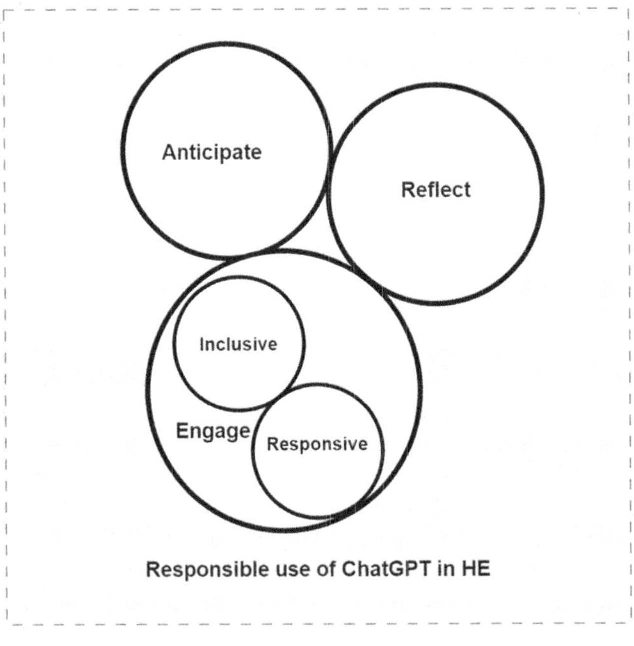

Fig. 6.2 Adapted RI framework for responsible use of ChatGPT in HE

and societal norms. Inclusiveness broadens the conversation, bringing diverse perspectives into the innovation process, thus enriching the development and application of ChatGPT in a way that respects and represents the wide array of stakeholders within the HE community. Lastly, responsiveness ensures that this approach remains dynamic and adaptable, capable of evolving with the changing needs and ethical considerations of society at large.

Together, these pillars of RRI creates a robust framework that supports the responsible integration of ChatGPT into the educational landscape. By blending anticipation, reflexivity, inclusiveness, and responsiveness, institutions can navigate the complexities of digital innovation in a manner that is both ethically grounded and socially beneficial. This holistic approach promotes not only consistent engagement with technological advancements but also ensures that such engagement is constructive, inclusive, and responsive to the diverse needs and challenges of the higher education community. An extensive RRI toolkit to guide the implementation of RRI principles across a wide range of scenarios (excluding the use of LLs in HE) is available at https://rri-tools.eu/. In the next section, we propose a simple step-by-step guide that most stakeholders will find useful.

6.7 How to Use GenAI Responsibly in HE: A Responsible Innovation Approach

When considering the use of Large Language Models such as ChatGPT for teaching and learning in higher education, it is essential to take a thoughtful approach that encompasses the principles of Responsible Research and Innovation (RRI). The process begins by **anticipating** both the positive and negative implications of such technology's deployment.

On the one hand, we must **identify the negatives**, acknowledging the risks associated with the use of GenAIs—these could include issues related to academic integrity, privacy, data security, bias, and the potential erosion of critical thinking skills. On the other hand, it is equally important to **identify the positives**, recognising the values ChatGPT brings, such as personalised learning, increased access to information, and potential for enhancing creativity and problem-solving skills.

Once we have identified these implications, we move on to **assess the controls** in place, such as existing policies and guidelines. This involves understanding at what levels these controls operate, whether at the module, programme, or university level. If the current control mechanisms are not adequately measuring something significant, we engage in a reflective process to determine what should be measured, how, and when. This might include metrics related to usage patterns, student engagement, or learning outcomes.

The next step is to **engage with the target stakeholders**. This requires identifying who they are and how we can engage them in a manner that is inclusive and represents the diverse voices within the HE community. It is important to consider how the use of LLMs fits into larger sectoral or national frameworks that may influence HE policies and practices.

This engagement leads to **improvement**—based on feedback and reflection, we aim to enhance the implementation strategy for LLMs. This could involve updating policies, offering training for faculty and students, and developing best practices for integrating ChatGPT into the curriculum.

Finally, we circle back to **respond**. This involves looking at the metrics we've gathered and interpreting what they tell us about the impact of ChatGPT on the educational process. The metrics inform us whether the risks are being mitigated effectively and whether the values we aimed to multiply are indeed being realised. If the data indicates success, we can further optimise and expand our approach. If not, we engage in a cycle of reflection and engagement, seeking to understand how we can better align our use of ChatGPT with the principles of RRI.

In this manner, the process becomes cyclical: **anticipating** outcomes, **reflecting** on practice, **engaging** stakeholders, **responding** to evidence, and seeking continuous **improvement**. By adhering to this methodology, HE institutions can ensure the responsible use of ChatGPT, balancing innovation with ethical considerations and societal needs.

While this narrative above is hypothetical, it suggests a pragmatic and holistic approach to the responsible use of generative AI in Higher Education (HE). It can also serve as a benchmark for HE institutions to evaluate where they stand in the journey toward the responsible use of GenAI (Fig. 6.3).

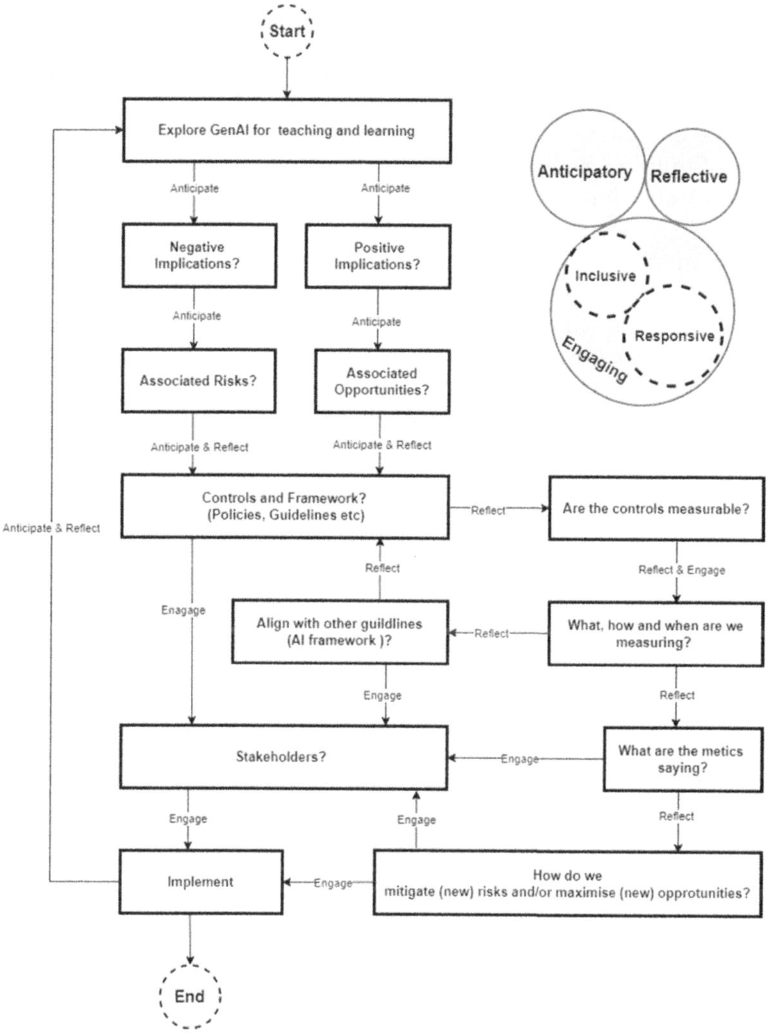

Fig. 6.3 Responsible GenAI4HE Flowchart

6.8 Conclusion

The integration of generative AI, like ChatGPT, into higher education (HE) presents an unparalleled opportunity to enhance the teaching and learning ecosystem. This chapter has traversed the multifaceted landscape of utilising generative AI within HEIs, emphasising the importance of responsible innovation to navigate the ethical, social, and technical complexities inherent in this digital transformation.

The unfolding interest among educators to incorporate tools like ChatGPT into their pedagogical practices, as revealed through surveys and discussions, underscores a collective aspiration to leverage AI's potential. However, this enthusiasm is tempered by legitimate concerns surrounding academic integrity, equity, and the preservation of critical thinking skills. The disparity between the interest in and actual usage of generative AI technologies in education highlights a cautious approach, prioritising responsibility over rapid adoption (Stahl, 2021; Stahl et al., 2023).

In addressing these concerns, the chapter has outlined a Responsible Research and Innovation (RRI) framework that offers a holistic approach to the ethical integration of generative AI in HE. This framework comprises four cornerstone principles: anticipation, reflexivity, inclusiveness, and responsiveness, each playing a pivotal role in fostering an ethical, equitable, and effective educational environment.

- **Anticipation** calls for a proactive stance, preparing for both the challenges and opportunities presented by generative AI. This forward-looking perspective is not about predicting the future with precision but about being prepared for various plausible futures. The anticipation of risks such as bias, misinformation, and academic integrity issues necessitates a multifaceted approach to mitigation, emphasising the need for continuous dialogue and adaptation.
- **Reflexivity** demands a critical self-examination of the roles, assumptions, and actions of all stakeholders involved in the innovation ecosystem. By reflecting on the broader context in which AI is deployed, educators, policymakers, and technologists can align their practices with societal values and educational goals. This continuous process of reflection ensures that the use of generative AI remains aligned with the principles of responsible innovation.

- **Inclusiveness** stresses the importance of engaging a diverse range of stakeholders in the innovation process. By democratising the conversation around AI in education, we can ensure that a broad spectrum of perspectives and values is considered, enriching the development and application of these technologies. Such an inclusive approach not only addresses concerns of equity and accessibility but also leverages the collective intelligence of the community to steer innovation towards societal benefit.
- **Responsiveness** highlights the need for innovation systems to be adaptable, and capable of responding to emerging societal needs and ethical considerations. This requires mechanisms for integrating societal values into innovation practices, ensuring that generative AI tools like ChatGPT are used in ways that reflect educational goals and societal expectations.

The intersection of these principles forms the foundation for a pragmatic Responsible Innovation approach to using GenAIs in HE. By embracing these guiding principles, HEIs can navigate the complexities of digital innovation, ensuring that the deployment of generative AI technologies like ChatGPT is both responsible and beneficial.

As we look to the future, the path forward requires not only adherence to these principles but also an ongoing commitment to dialogue, collaboration, and adaptation. The dynamic nature of technology and society means that what constitutes responsible use today may evolve tomorrow. Therefore, HEIs must remain vigilant, continuously assessing and adjusting their practices in response to new insights, challenges, and opportunities.

In conclusion, the responsible use of generative AI in higher education is not merely an aspirational goal but a necessary commitment to ensuring that technological innovation serves to enhance, rather than diminish, the quality and integrity of education. By fostering an environment of anticipation, reflexivity, inclusiveness, and responsiveness, we can harness the transformative potential of generative AI to create an educational landscape that is equitable, ethical, and aligned with the enduring values of academic excellence. The journey towards responsible innovation is ongoing, and each step forward enriches our collective understanding and capability to shape a future where technology and humanity converge in the service of education and societal progress.

References

Margherita, N., & Bernd, S. (2018). RRI in higher education. *The ORBIT Journal, 1*(4), 1–8. https://doi.org/10.29297/orbit.v1i4.78

OpenAI Community. (2023). *Exploring emotional connections in human-AI interactions*. Retrieved from https://community.openai.com/t/exploring-emotional-connections-in-human-ai-interactions/281770

Stahl, B. C. (2021). *Artificial intelligence for a better future an ecosystem perspective on the ethics of AI and emerging digital technologies*. http://www.springer.com/series/13811

Stahl, B. C., Schroeder, D., & Rodrigues, R. (2023). *Ethics of artificial intelligence case studies and options for addressing ethical challenges SpringerBriefs in research and innovation governance* (Vol. 1).

Stilgoe, J., Owen, R., & Macnaghten, P. (2013). Developing a framework for responsible innovation. *Research Policy, 42*(9), 1568–1580. https://doi.org/10.1016/j.respol.2013.05.008

Tarisayi Kudzayi. (2024). ChatGPT use in universities in South Africa through a socio-technical lens. *Cogent Education, 11*(1), 2295654. https://doi.org/10.1080/2331186X.2023.2295654

Xiao, P., Chen, Y., & Bao, W. (2023). *Waiting, banning, and embracing: An empirical analysis of adapting policies for generative AI in higher education*. https://www.celt.iastate.edu/resources/ai-teach-learn/

CHAPTER 7

Emergent Issues and Future Considerations

7.1 Introduction

In the preceding six chapters, we first set out the general case for application of generative AI (GenAI) for teaching and learning in Higher Education (HE). From there, we discussed specific use cases across a wide range of teaching and learning activities, including lesson preparation and content development, key considerations in developing personalised learning, and applications in formative and summative learning and assessment. In this chapter, we offer reflections on the three areas that will underpin future successful applications of GenAI in the higher education sector and some key risks that stakeholders must consider while integrating GenAI into higher education.

7.2 Key Areas for Future GenAI Success in Higher Education

Educators Must Learn to Live with Generative AI

The first point to re-iterate is that GenAI will not go away. Educators in HE must embrace the challenge and harness the opportunities it offers to strengthen their practice for improved outcomes for learners. There are three major reasons for this imperative.

The first is an obvious one: GenAI is now ubiquitous, and students are active users regardless of whether they are advised to use it or not

A. Owoseni et al., *Generative AI in Higher Education*,
https://doi.org/10.1007/978-3-031-60179-8_7

use it. In a sense, GenAI is a something of an unstoppable moving train, but inherently a value-free tool that can nevertheless be deployed in a right or wrong way, for good or ill. Imposing an outright ban is a fool's errand, in the circumstances. Educators can influence how it is used, but only if they engage with it themselves. In this book, we have highlighted a number of positive use cases, but these are by no means exhaustive. The burgeoning field of AI lends itself to a wide variety of innovative applications. It is a fertile field for engaged creative minds. Educators who refuse to engage with AI are unlikely to be of help to learners using it and seeking guidance on how to use it correctly and appropriately to enrich their learning experience.

The second reason is that AI is already shaping the world of work. The last edition of the Future of Jobs Report 2023 indicates that majority of organisations are adopting AI, and most are investing resources to train and re-train their workers to use AI in their operations. More and more roles in the future will require some competence in artificial intelligence, as well as other frontier digital technologies. Educators, who are training learners for the twenty-first-century job market, cannot afford to be left behind. If Industry demands it, educators must be prepared to supply it. Furthermore, curriculum design and teaching delivery in HE is increasingly collaborative, and industry partners are increasingly sought to make inputs to new module designs and content delivery. Individual educators should therefore have requisite competence to engage meaningfully with industry partners and provide effective support for learners.

The third reason is that frontier technologies, such as GenAI's, will inevitably shape educators' practice, as teachers and researchers. This is the case with previous iterations of technologies that are now considered mainstream in the HE sectors. One example is VLE technologies, now a mainstay in HE sectors. More recently, following the outbreak of COVID-19 pandemic, collaborative software like Zoom and MS Teams have become indispensable tools for universities and colleges, facilitating seamless transition to online and hybrid learning models, with synchronous and asynchronous contents (Imran et al., 2023; Turnbull et al., 2021). Like these technologies, GenAI is poised to play increasingly prominent, and ultimately central, role in the higher education sector. Educators should prepare early for that "inevitability" by developing competences on the use of AI both for their own research and teaching practice. As we have highlighted in this book, the use of AI can drive efficiency in various teaching activities including content preparation, development of engaging tasks, and activities for learners. GenAI can also be used to support research in areas such as language editing, and time-intensive activities like data cleaning and processing, presentation of results, management of international collaboration, and public communication of research via multiple channels, including social media.

We now turn our attention to competency. In order for educators to "live" with GenAI, they must develop requisite competencies and skills. They do not have to be top-of-the-range proficiency, but just enough to set themselves for lifelong learning and evolution. Below, we highlight some practical suggestions for educators to develop these AI skills:

- **Set up a free account:** The first suggested action point is to set up a free account for a GenAI product. Following Open AI's pioneering launch in November 2022, other major actors have stepped in with similar products, including Google's Gemini (formerly Bard) and Microsoft Co-Pilot, among others. Setting up an account provides you with the immediate opportunity to explore and learn more about GenAI. You can make it a fun start by introducing yourself and ask your GenAI to advise where best to start as a new educator signing up for the first time (see Prompt 7.1 below).

Prompt 7.1: Educator—Making a Start with ChatGPT

ChatGPT Prompt

Hello. I am a Professor in Entrepreneurship at a UK university trying to find out what ChatGPT is all about and if it can be of significant use for me as an educator. I just signed up to this platform and wondering where to start, or whether I should start, here. Do you have any suggestions?

ChatGPT Response

Hello! Welcome to the platform, and it's great to hear that you're interested in exploring how ChatGPT can support your work as an educator in entrepreneurship. There are indeed many ways in which ChatGPT can be of use to you:

- **Research Assistance**: ChatGPT can help you with research tasks by providing information on various topics related to entrepreneurship, business trends, case studies, and more.

- **Student Support:** You can leverage ChatGPT to provide additional support to your students. It can assist them with homework, clarifying concepts, generating ideas, or even simulating business scenarios.
- **Content Creation:** ChatGPT can aid in generating content for lectures, assignments, or course materials. It can assist in writing explanations, creating examples, or even generating discussion prompts.
- **Q&A Sessions:** You can use ChatGPT during Q&A sessions to provide instant answers to student queries, thereby enhancing engagement and interaction.
- **Feedback Generation:** ChatGPT can help in generating feedback for student assignments, providing constructive criticism, and suggesting areas of improvement.

  To get started, you can try engaging with ChatGPT in various ways:
- **Ask Questions:** Feel free to ask any questions you have about entrepreneurship, education, or any other topic relevant to your interests.
- **Test Responses:** Experiment with different types of questions or prompts to see how ChatGPT responds.
- **Explore Features:** Familiarize yourself with the platform's features, such as document summarization, text completion, and conversation mode.
- **Join Communities:** Engage with other educators or professionals on the platform to share experiences, tips, and best practices.

If you have any specific questions or tasks in mind, feel free to ask, and I'll do my best to assist you!

ChatGPT Screen

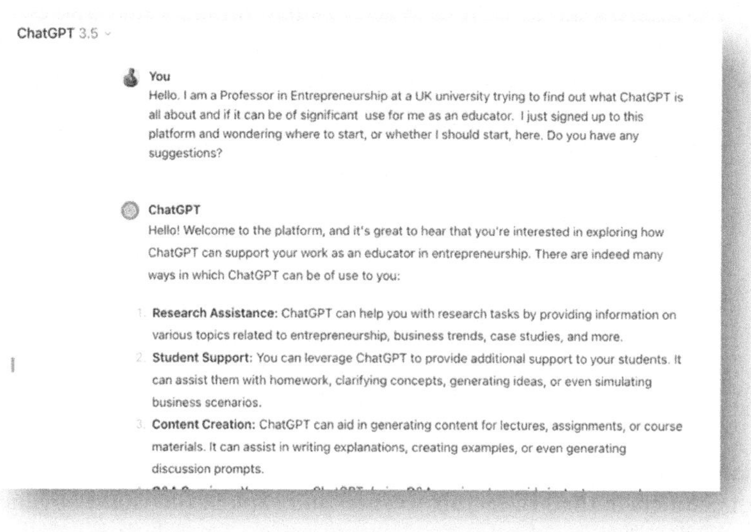
ChatGPT 3.5

You

Hello. I am a Professor in Entrepreneurship at a UK university trying to find out what ChatGPT is all about and if it can be of significant use for me as an educator. I just signed up to this platform and wondering where to start, or whether I should start, here. Do you have any suggestions?

ChatGPT

Hello! Welcome to the platform, and it's great to hear that you're interested in exploring how ChatGPT can support your work as an educator in entrepreneurship. There are indeed many ways in which ChatGPT can be of use to you:

1. **Research Assistance:** ChatGPT can help you with research tasks by providing information on various topics related to entrepreneurship, business trends, case studies, and more.
2. **Student Support:** You can leverage ChatGPT to provide additional support to your students. It can assist them with homework, clarifying concepts, generating ideas, or even simulating business scenarios.
3. **Content Creation:** ChatGPT can aid in generating content for lectures, assignments, or course materials. It can assist in writing explanations, creating examples, or even generating discussion prompts.

- **Join fora of fellow practitioners:** The next recommendation, and ChatGPT also suggests this by the way, is to join groups of fellow generative AI users. There are all-purpose groups like ChatGPT suggests above, where you can interact with professionals from a broad spectrum of sectors including but not limited to HE. This can help you to learn about other creative use cases outside of higher education. There are also groups dedicated specifically to exploring applications of AI in higher education. This can help you to dig deeper into different creative use cases and new opportunities to deploy AI to strengthen curricular and enrich the learning experience of students. If there is no such group in your university, you can start one. It is always useful to have a local group of GenAI practitioners with whom you can share and explore new ideas. There are also global platforms, like AI-Ed (AI Education) that focuses on the intersection of artificial intelligence and education. In addition, platforms like LinkedIn and Reddit often host discussions on cutting-edge applications of generative AI in the higher education contexts. We believe this school of thought is influencing the recently announced ChatGPT Edu by OpenAI, an attempt to encapsulate all use cases into a digital product for accessibility, effectiveness, and productivity.

- **Attend seminars and workshops regularly:** Regular participation in online platforms and groups can be complemented with attendance at seminars and workshops. Workshops tend to be more focused on specific sub-topics and use cases, and you can select the ones that match your particular interest at a time. Seminars are also a good way to keep abreast of the latest developments, especially those relating to policy at national and sector levels. Typically, seminars feature more proficient and expert users sharing their knowledge and experience and responding to specific questions and issues participants want to explore. Workshops and seminars also provide excellent networking opportunities for HE practitioners.

The overall message here is that there are many opportunities out there for beginners in the HE sectors to enter and explore the world of generative AI. It offers benefits for them as educators to enrich their practice in curriculum development and learning engagement. It also offers opportunities for them as researchers looking to enhance their effectiveness and productivity as knowledge producers. In other words, generative AI enables HE practitioners to raise their productivity in the mutually reinforcing domains of research and teaching, for the overall benefit of both themselves and their learners.

Users Must Take Personal Responsibility for the Use of Generative AI

So far, the use cases and prompts explored in this book have re-established a well-known fact: GenAI stands out for its remarkable ability to generate new, previously unseen outputs based on the data it has been trained on. This capability can revolutionise higher education by enhancing creativity, automating content generation, and providing personalised learning experiences. These benefits are undeniable, yet the use of this technology especially by individual users requires a cautious approach to prevent misuse and unintended consequences. While its potential to transform learning is unquestionable, its power necessitates a parallel emphasis on responsible and ethical use. We argue that, in the hands of students and educators alike, GenAI must be wielded with a profound sense of ethical responsibility to maintain academic integrity, foster critical thinking, and ensure a fair and equitable learning environment. GenAI is a double-edged sword that can be exploited for malicious purposes, such as creating deepfakes, spreading misinformation, or the production of illegal content. Beyond these surface-level concerns, deeper ethical issues relate to intellectual property (IP) rights and academic integrity.

As AI-generated content becomes increasingly indistinguishable from human-created content, distinguishing between the two and determining ownership becomes challenging. Users must respect existing IP rights and consider the implications of using AI to generate derivative works. Establishing clear guidelines and legal frameworks concerning the ownership of AI-generated content is crucial to protect creators' rights and encourage innovation within ethical boundaries.

The World Intellectual Property Organization (WIPO), a global forum for intellectual property policy, services, information, and cooperation, has publicly acknowledged these concerns. They have noted that: GenAI presents many IP touchpoints and uncertainties. While it is impossible to completely mitigate these IP risks, the following considerations may be useful for users navigating IP considerations in this evolving domain. Employers (and students) of HE institutions using generative AI tools may inadvertently reveal trade secrets or waive confidentiality in commercially sensitive information if such information is used for prompting GenAI tools. To prevent this, they should consider leveraging a combination of technical, legal, and practical safeguards (WIPO, 2024).

For instance, a use case that is relatable to this context is in Chapter 3, where we developed the circular plastic economy GPT, which was customised and "trained" with a sixteen-chapter textbook which is an output from a UKRI-sponsored research project. In this case, the book that was used in an open access book available for use by all. However, educators looking to implement similar model in the future need to pay close attention to intellectual property rights, and ensure they fully acknowledge their sources. Additionally, there is significant legal uncertainty regarding whether the use of GenAI tools, their training, and outputs constitute IP infringements, with answers varying by jurisdiction. Users should mitigate risks by seeking indemnities where possible, vetting datasets that are used for building GPTs, and implementing technical and other practical measures moderated by policies to minimise the likelihood of infringement. According to WIPO (2024), there are pending litigations worldwide which aim to determine whether training AI with IP-protected items, the use of such trained AI models, and the outputs they generate amount to IP infringements.

HE Institutions Must Adapt and Keep Pace

In today's teaching and learning environment as well as the broader labour market, the demarcation between uniquely human capabilities and routine automatable tasks is fluid. In this context, HE institutions should seek to help learners develop skills that are complemented by, not contrasted with, AI including creativity, complex problem-solving, articulate communication, teamwork, flexibility, and ethical discernment. Broadly speaking, it is futile to resist the potential impact of GenAI tools on teaching and learning processes. Rather, institutions should proactively engage with these tools in order to tackle emerging challenges and devise strategies for their innovative and responsible application. The proactive engagement that we advocate here leaves no room for hypocrisy where universities ban the use of GenAI and yet seek to attract research funding on the application of AI technology in education. It also precludes the one-sided paternalistic approach where education practitioners and stakeholders only seek to regulate what others, including students, do with the technology but fail to improve themselves. Rather, we advocate that HE institutions adapt and keep pace with the technology. This is important because of the intrinsic nature of knowledge and learning, the two phenomena that underlie all technologies and their applications.

Firstly, knowledge is both dynamic and transient; in other words, it constantly evolves to the point of becoming obsolete over time. This characteristic of knowledge necessitates a continuous commitment to learning and adaptation. Secondly, knowledge is cumulative, that is, new knowledge builds upon existing knowledge such that learning and adaptation become easier over time. These two features of knowledge suggest that it leads to greater benefits over time but offers only short windows of opportunity to take advantage of those benefits. For example, decades ago educators would be celebrated for expertise in teaching the use of slide rules to solve problems in logarithms. Today, that knowledge has very limited value.

The challenge for HE institutions is to position themselves to capitalise on the opportunities that GenAI offers before the technology goes beyond reach. In the rapidly evolving knowledge landscape, resistance, hesitation, or delay in adoption and adaptation spells obsolescence. By the time laggards recognise and react to the emerging trends, early adopters will have already established a formidable knowledge advantage that could perpetuate or widen the gap between them and the rest. Therefore, we recommend that every institution should seek to secure a position close to the top of the summit before it becomes insurmountably steep. Institutions that fail to respond could be left behind—it is as simple.

This recommendation is even more important given the rapid rate at which GenAI tools emerge and evolve. For example, over the space of two weeks during May 2024, OpenAI released a new flagship model (GPT-4o), made more capabilities (including custom GPTs, data analysis, and web surfing, among others) available for free in ChatGPT, and announced ChatGPT Edu. ChatGPT Edu was specifically tailored for universities and offers enhanced AI capabilities, ranging from advanced data analytics to support for a wide spectrum of administrative and academic tasks. For instance, custom GPT models can be readily developed within the ChatGPT Edu environment to facilitate language learning, grant application processes, personalised academic support, and many more. This is a reflection of how the future might look like. The HE institution of the future will need to take decisive action today by investing in capacity building, ICT infrastructure, collaboration, and risk management.

7.3 Key Risks of GenAI Integration into Higher Education

In this section, we highlight a few important risks that HE institutions and stakeholders need to consider when developing strategies for integrating GenAI into higher education.

Risk of Plagiarism and Academic Dishonesty

The ability of GenAIs to produce text indistinguishable from human output introduces profound concerns regarding plagiarism and the erosion of academic integrity. Imagine a student facing a looming deadline for a research paper. Exhausted and overwhelmed, they turn to a GenAI tool, feeding it a topic and letting it produce a seemingly complete essay. While this scenario might seem tempting, it poses a significant threat to academic integrity. HE institutions bear the fundamental responsibility of upholding rigorous standards, and the indiscriminate use of GenAI undermines the essence of education: fostering independent thought, research skills, and critical analysis. Although plagiarism detection tools have evolved, current AI text detection tools have not been consistently effective in identifying AI-generated texts. In fact, some studies have shown that texts written by non-native English speakers have been incorrectly identified as AI-generated. Universities will, without doubt, implement measures to detect AI-generated content, and the consequences of such discoveries can be severe, potentially leading to failing grades or even expulsion.

The true value of higher education lies not only in acquiring knowledge but also in cultivating the ability to think critically and ask probing questions. Generative AI, by providing ready-made essays or code, risks becoming a crutch that impedes the development of these crucial skills. Students who rely solely on AI-generated outputs may find it challenging to grasp the underlying concepts, analyse arguments, or form their own well-reasoned opinions. Engaging with a problem, exploring different perspectives, and constructing a coherent argument are integral to the learning process. Circumventing this process through GenAI not only detracts from the educational experience but may also inadequately prepares graduates for the complexities of the real world.

Indeed, the risk of students delegating their academic duties to AI and thereby circumventing genuine learning opportunities is widely acknowledged. This risk is compounded by the limitations of traditional plagiarism detection tools like Turnitin in identifying AI-generated content. The recommended response is a paradigm shift in assessment towards evaluating critical thinking and original contributions. The focus must pivot from rote learning to the demonstration of analytical abilities, creative synthesis, and application of information in novel contexts. The paradigm needs to shift away from formats susceptible to AI replication (essays, for instance) towards innovative assessment forms, such as open-ended exams, scenario-based tasks, portfolios, and projects that test individual insight.

No doubt, GenAI is a powerful tool with the potential to enhance learning. However, it is just that—a tool, not a substitute for the irreplaceable role of educators and the dedication required from students. By using GenAI responsibly and ethically, we can minimise the associated risks and strike a balance that upholds the standard and integrity of the academic experience. In reality, the future of higher education depends on striking this delicate balance, ensuring that technology acts as a springboard for learning rather than a shortcut that undermines its foundational principles.

Risks of Biases and Inequality

By design, GenAI is trained on extensive datasets that inadvertently ingrain biases, mirror societal disparities, and amplify historical inequities. Thus, adopting these models without caution could perpetuate stereotypes, foster discrimination, disseminate misinformation, exacerbate social inequities and contravene the foundational principles of HE. These challenges are well known and should be accounted for in the response strategy of HE institutions. For example, clear guidelines should be established for the ethical use of AI tools, including rigorous vetting processes to identify and mitigate biases before integrating them into educational tools. As vendors of virtual learning environments (VLEs) and educational software-as-a service (SaaS) solutions continue to embed AI functionalities within their products, HE institutions need to interrogate the fairness, transparency, inclusivity, and transparency of these functionalities. Specifically, HE institutions need to insist on algorithmic transparency and accountability. HE institutions may also implement procurement protocols that mandate comprehensive impact assessments for AI tools.

Moreover, there are wide disparities in access to cutting-edge AI tools and the requisite computing resources across different contexts. This threatens to create a socioeconomic divide or widen it within educational settings. Consequently, the education system could become a bifurcated one where access to AI tools becomes a symbol of privilege. HE institutions need to actively cooperate to overcome this challenge that could undermine the egalitarian ethos of HE. For example, HE institutions can develop partnerships with technology companies and non-profit organisations to provide wider access to AI tools and necessary computing resources. Such partnerships can implement initiatives like shared cloud computing access, donation of AI software licenses, and establishment of AI resource hubs. Moreover, training and education programmes for both students and faculty in underserved communities can empower them to use AI tools effectively.

GenAI has the potential to deepen existing inequities in educational access and outcomes. An illustrative example involves AI tools used for language learning, which might be calibrated to standard dialects, thereby disadvantaging students who speak in regional accents or dialects not recognised by the AI. Similarly, historical data used in GenAI algorithms could reflect societal biases, thereby skewing learning content away from a diverse and inclusive curriculum. Therefore, the development and deployment of GenAI-driven pedagogies must undergo continuous auditing for biases that might disadvantage minority communities or reinforce stereotypes. For example, AI-enhanced content for history lessons should be vetted to include diverse perspectives and contributions from various cultures, avoiding Eurocentric or other biased viewpoints. In striving for equity, it is crucial for educators and technology developers to collaborate on creating AI tools that are adaptable to different learning styles and needs. Such adaptable innovations will support all students in reaching their full potential.

Risks of AI Illiteracy and Mental Redundancy

There is a pressing AI literacy imperative. The challenges associated with the use of AI in education can only be effectively confronted by competent administrators, educators, and other practitioners. This creates a pressing need to enhance the AI literacy of HE stakeholders. Before they can engage responsibly and innovatively with them, both students and educators need to develop an astute understanding of AI tools—encompassing their operational mechanisms, limitations, biases, and ethical considerations. For instance, training for administrators, teachers, and students on the potential pitfalls and ethical considerations of using GenAIs is practically non-negotiable. Moreover, training programmes are needed to equip educators with strategies for using AI as a supplement rather than a substitute for traditional teaching methods. Furthermore, HE institutions should actively participate in ongoing research and discussions aimed at advancing knowledge of these technologies. After all, it is extremely difficult, if not impossible, to manage what is not understood.

Overreliance on AI could erode critical thinking. If students and teachers rely too much on AI for academic tasks, a dependency syndrome could emerge where the cultivation of critical analytical skills and independent thought is impaired. Thus, HE institutions need frameworks and protocols that help to balance AI-assisted teaching and learning with activities that promote autonomous reasoning and creativity. In this regard, blended learning models are a promising alternative because they integrate AI tools for specific tasks while reserving significant portions of the curriculum for problem-based learning, discussions, and projects that require independent analysis and creative thought. Additionally, assessment criteria could be adjusted to reward critical thinking and originality as way to incentivise students to develop and demonstrate real learning.

HE institutions need to be proactive, inclusive, and future-oriented in policy formulation. The responsibility of HE institutions in dealing with the implications of AI extends to the formulation of explicit, transparent policies governing AI use in education. The policies should provide guidelines to curb misuse, set parameters for ethical usage, and define the specifications for integrating AI into teaching and learning. At the same time, the policies should not create a constraint to experimentation and capacity building. Clearly, the task of formulating the right policies is not trivial. This is why it is important for HE institutions to be proactive by anticipating areas of policy needs and responding on time, rather than waiting to use policies as a reactive tool. Moreover, it is essential to have open dialogue within and beyond the academic community in order to foster a collective ethos of responsible AI utilisation. For instance, the perspective of students is instrumental to creating inclusive AI policies. In addition, today's HE institutions need to understand their role as preparing learners not only for today's labour market but also for the future where existing competencies may become irrelevant and new skills may be in demand. Policies around the use of AI in HE should reflect this future orientation.

7.4 Towards a Responsible AI-Enhanced Higher Education Ecosystem

The responsible use of generative AI in higher education should be an important concern for all relevant stakeholders. As already discussed in Chapter 6, responsible GenAI use can be built upon the Responsible Research and Innovation (RRI) framework. The framework emphasises anticipatory, reflective, inclusive, and responsive approaches to innovation such that technological advancements align with societal values and needs. This has several implications for the wider HE ecosystem.

First and foremost, HE institutions must develop clear guidelines for the responsible use of GenAI tools. These guidelines should specify acceptable applications, such as utilising GenAI for brainstorming sessions or generating preliminary outlines, and unequivocally ban its use for producing plagiarised work. For example, a university could implement a policy where GenAI-generated content must be clearly labelled and used solely for ideation, a draft or starting point for teaching, learning, or research and development.

Secondly, educators play a crucial role in integrating discussions about AI ethics within their curriculum. This can take the form of case studies on AI misuse, debates on the ethical use of AI in academic settings, or analysis of real-world scenarios where AI's impact on society is examined. For instance, a course could include a module where students debate the ethics of using AI in creating art or literature, critically examining questions of originality and creativity.

Promoting a culture of academic integrity is essential. By valuing original thought, critical inquiry, and honest effort above all, educators can foster an environment where students are motivated to excel through their intellectual pursuits. An example action could be rewarding students who demonstrate innovative approaches to combining AI-generated content with their unique insights, thereby encouraging responsible AI use that complements human creativity. Educators wearing their researcher hats should also model ethical behaviour in their use of GenAIs, for example in manuscript preparation. Most academic publishers now acknowledge that researchers use GenAI in some form in the process of undertaking research and disseminating output. Publishers distinguish between copy writing, which requires original content creation and creative thinking; and copy-editing, which involves reviewing and correcting already written material to improve accuracy and readability. As such, most journal guidelines now include warnings that use of GenAI for copy writing is unacceptable and unethical but use for copy-editing is permissible. Emerald Publishing (2023) observes, this is because use of GenAI tool "mirrors standard tools already employed to improve spelling and grammar, and uses existing author-created material, rather than generating wholly new content, while the authors(s) remain responsible for the original work".

The responsible and ethical use of GenAI transcends mere recommendation; it is a necessity as the technology landscape continues to evolve. Today's decisions and indecisions will significantly influence how GenAI impacts teaching and learning, and by extension the society. Key action points include:

- Understanding generative AI: Educators and students should be well informed about the opportunities, risks, and limitations associated with generative AI. Workshops or seminars could be conducted to disseminate knowledge on these topics.
- Blending human creativity with AI outputs: Encouraging the integration of human input and creativity with AI outputs ensures that the ownership of final works remains clear. Collaborative projects could exemplify how AI can augment rather than replacing human creativity.
- Respecting intellectual property: Avoiding the use of third-party intellectual property in AI prompts can minimise the risk of generating infringing content. Legal workshops could help clarify what constitutes fair use and how to navigate copyright considerations.
- Safeguarding confidential information: It is crucial to avoid using confidential or sensitive information in AI prompts. Training sessions on data privacy could help staff and students recognise and protect personal and institutional data.
- Providing clear and transparent documentation: Staff and students should be encouraged to label GenAI-generated outputs and maintain records of AI prompts used. This could be part of a broader policy on academic honesty and transparency.
- Steering clear of deepfake technologies: The use of deepfake or other potentially deceptive AI technologies should be explicitly prohibited. Ethical guidelines should address the implications of creating and distributing such content.
- Communicating legal risk: Clearly communicating the legal risks associated with generative AI use helps align practices with the institution's risk appetite. Legal teams could provide regular updates on evolving laws and regulations affecting AI use.

7.5 Concluding Thoughts

We have, in this final chapter, highlighted a number of key issues relating to the future of generative AI, in relation to HE practitioners, general users, and at organisational and institutional levels. This underlines the multi-layered and multi-dimensional future of generative AI, and why stakeholders must work together to harness GenAI's true potentials in higher education. In effect, responsibility for ethical use of GenAI is shared, and each stakeholder must play their part. Educators need to keep updated and stay at the cutting edge of the technology, in order to be of better value to learners, but also for themselves as researchers and knowledge producers. General users should be aware of their responsibilities to use AI tools ethically, and their liabilities for unethical and malicious use. Stakeholders, including HE institutions, must be proactive in creating clear guidelines and policies for the responsible and ethical use of GenAI, while also supporting its use through continuous training of staff. Additionally, it is crucial to provide an enabling environment to maximise opportunities and mitigate risks associated with GenAI.

The future of AI is as promising as it is fraught with risks. Both the opportunities and challenges are inevitable, and a "Luddite" resistance to the technology is ultimately a fool's errand. HE practitioners should embrace the exciting opportunity to shape the use of AI and other frontier digital technologies. An open-minded approach will not only help to enrich the learning experience of students, but it will also enhance the productivity of HE practitioners as knowledge producers.

References

Emerald Publishing. (2023). *Emerald Publishing's stance on AI tools in content creation and peer review*. Retrieved from https://www.emeraldgrouppublishing.com/news-and-press-releases/emerald-publishings-stance-ai-tools-content-creation-and-peer-review

Imran, R., Fatima, A., Elbayoumi Salem, I., & Allil, K. (2023). Teaching and learning delivery modes in higher education: Looking back to move forward post-COVID-19 era. *International Journal of Management Education*. https://doi.org/10.1016/j.ijme.2023.100805

Turnbull, D., Chugh, R., & Luck, J. (2021). Transitioning to E-Learning during the COVID-19 pandemic: How have Higher Education Institutions responded to the challenge? *Education and Information Technologies, 26*(5), 6401–6419. https://doi.org/10.1007/s10639-021-10633-w

World Intellectual Property Organization (WIPO). (2024). *Generative AI: navigating intellectual property IP and frontier technologies*. https://www.wipo.int/export/sites/www/about-ip/en/frontier_technologies/pdf/generative-ai-factsheet.pdf

Index

A. Owoseni et al., *Generative AI in Higher Education*,
https://doi.org/10.1007/978-3-031-60179-8

SPRINGER NATURE

GPSR Compliance

The European Union's (EU) General Product Safety Regulation (GPSR) is a set of rules that requires consumer products to be safe and our obligations to ensure this.

If you have any concerns about our products, you can contact us on ProductSafety@springernature.com

In case Publisher is established outside the EU, the EU authorized representative is:

Springer Nature Customer Service Center GmbH
Europaplatz 3
69115 Heidelberg, Germany

The manufacturer's authorised representative in the EU is Springer Nature Customer Service Centre GmbH, Europaplatz 3, 69115 Heidelberg, Germany. If you have any concerns regarding our products, please contact ProductSafety@springernature.com

Printed and bound by CPI Group (UK) Ltd, Croydon, CR0 4YY
30/09/2026
02225595-0002